# SLAVE GENEALOGY:
# A RESEARCH GUIDE
# WITH CASE STUDIES

by

David H. Streets

# HERITAGE BOOKS, INC.

HERITAGE BOOKS, INC.
3602 Maureen Lane, Bowie, MD 20715
Phone (301)-464-1159


ISBN 0-917890-63-9

A Complete Catalog
Listing Several Hundred Titles
on History, Genealogy & Americana
Free on Request

# TABLE OF CONTENTS

# LIST OF GENEALOGICAL CHARTS

# LIST OF TABLES

# INTRODUCTION

Over the past few years we have seen the field of family history capture the interest and imagination of a much broader segment of the American population, awakening in the American people a seemingly insatiable desire to discover, understand and preserve their personal and cultural heritages. In response to this phenomenon, American family historians have been virtually flooded with studies and guides to assist them in their personal quests into the past. The range of source materials available, while varying greatly in quality, is almost limitless in quantity.

Relatively few of the source materials now available to the family historian, however, are of any practical value to black Americans, and this important segment of the American family has often been left out. Although many excellent genealogical guide books mention the special problems involved in tracing black slave ancestry, few provide any practical advice or offer examples on how to approach these special problems. With few exceptions, most American genealogical studies to date have been directed towards Americans of European ancestry, while the genealogies of millions of Americans of African ancestry have been ignored.

Just as there is no single approach to the study of Family History for all white Americans, so too, there is no single approach which can encompass the historical experiences of all black families. Many different circumstances and settings must be considered. While slavery is not the heritage of all black Americans, it is the ancestry of most. This book examines the unique circumstances faced by family historians who wish to trace black families through those years of slavery.

The conditions of slavery varied over time and in each state and territory. Although certain aspects of slavery were common to the lives of slaves everywhere, the life of each individual slave was as unique as his or her own person and was governed principally by the laws and customs of the community in which that slave was forced to live. The conditions of slavery on the large plantations in the cotton-belt states of the "Deep South" varied greatly from the conditions faced by slaves living on small family farms in the states of the "Upper South," and the records relating to the lives of these slaves reflect those differences. Just as it is necessary for historians interested in the histories of America's white families to familiarize themselves with the peculiarities of the communities of residence of their subjects, so too must historians researching slave families. The general guidelines presented in this book can provide useful assistance to all those interested in slave ancestry, but it must be remembered that the conditions of slavery did vary from one area to another, and it is necessary to adjust one's research accordingly.

In this book those slaves living on small farms rather than on large plantations have been chosen as the focus of examination. Contrary to a popular misconception, not all slaves labored in the fields or in the grand mansions of the large plantations. In fact, only half of the slaves in the South lived on "Plantations" with as many as 20 slaves, and only one-quarter of the slaves lived on large plantations which housed a workforce of at least 50 slaves [1]. While the large plantation has certainly become the most identifiable and imagined historical setting for American slavery, anyone interested in a more complete portrayal of slavery in America must consider the millions of slaves who lived either as the sole black inhabitant or in small units on the thousands of small farms and in small towns scattered throughout the slave states and territories. While these small farms were the actual historical setting for many of the slave ancestors of today's black Americans, little attention has been given to this side of the slavery experience.

What little research that has been done to date on slavery and slave families has almost entirely been done on slave families from several large plantations with surviving slave records (see endnotes 2-4). Considering the rich reservoir of information which can be extracted from those plantation ledgers which have been passed down intact, it is certainly understandable how they have become one of the principal resource tools on slavery and slave genealogy. These plantation records, however, are only one form of documentation available to the historian, and do not accurately reflect the lives of the millions of slaves who never experienced plantation life. For those interested in learning more about non-plantation slaves, a different road of investigation must be followed. It requires great patience, tenacity and more than a little ingenuity and luck. It is for the travelers down this often overlooked road of investigation that the findings in this book are offered as guideposts. By learning how to research the lives of these non-plantation slaves, new opportunities open up for a better understanding of the entire slavery experience.

This book examines several of the principal record sources available to the family historian to show how these records can be utilized to confront the unique circumstances and problems inherent in the researching of slave ancestors. Since most records of significance for the family historian are found at the county level, these local records are examined in detail. Probate records, vital records, tax records and the sundry array of documents found in the court order books and county deed books (bills of sale, deeds of gift, mortgages, records of importation and manumissions) are examined for the clues they provide concerning slaves, and practical examples are given to show how these various record groups can be utilized. To facilitate a more detailed examination of the potential uses of these county records, the discussions presented in this book are restricted to the records of one community, Wayne County, Kentucky.

Slavery also existed in the large cities, and many black family historians will eventually be able to trace some of their ancestors back to these early urban centers. Life in the city compelled slaves to adapt to yet another alternative lifestyle, and the experiences of those slaves forced to labor in the cities differed greatly from those who labored either on the large plantations or in small rural environs. Since these differing lifestyles experienced by the slaves resulted in differing modes of documenting their lives, a researcher must accommodate his research to the appropriate environment and corresponding documentation. Although the focus of investigation presented in this book is not directly related to these urban centers, the explanations and examples it presents can provide useful guidelines to the inquisitive researcher tracing slaves in any of the possible environments.

Regardless of where the bond of slavery may eventually have led its victims, it is a simple fact that the roots of almost all black Americans originate in Africa. It is a heritage which is remembered with pride. Alex Haley has shown that it is possible for some black Americans to trace their ancestry back to their immigrant African ancestor, and it is a goal which many black genealogists may eventually choose to pursue. This endeavor, however, is not a principal motivation behind the work presented here; this book does not deal with the African slave trade nor any aspects of it. It is the lives of the immigrant Africans' descendants, who with the passage of time ceased to be Africans and became Afro-Americans, who are the subjects of this investigation. By the eve of the Civil War, the descendants of less than 400,000 imported African slaves had become an integral, if not yet integrated part of the American population, numbering over 4,000,000 [5].

Slavery as an institution was an integral part of American life for over two hundred years. Americans of African ancestry, although doubly burdened by the bonds of slavery and anonymity, played an indispensable role in the opening of the ever-widening American frontier and in the development of the American nation. It is hoped that the information presented here will help many Afro-Americans to discover the role their own families played in that early drama, and in turn will broaden our vista of America's past.

While any study of slave ancestry is naturally set against the larger backdrop of slavery itself, this is not an historical study of the institution of slavery per se. The political, economic and social aspects of slavery are examined only from the perspective of their possible significance to the family historian interested in identifying slave ancestors. For a better understanding of that ancestry, however, one should engage in at least a limited survey of the institution and the significant impact that it exerted on American culture and society.

Much has been written about slavery and about the lives of the slaves. Foes and supporters, condemners and apologists, can all find works to defend and corroborate their particular opinions about the "merits" of the slave system. Indeed, with such a vast and wide-ranging reservoir of material available on the subject, it is difficult sometimes to know where to search for the truth.

Until the late 1950's and early 1960's, most treatises on slavery were devoted either to arguing the merits of the system or to discussing how it had changed and manipulated the slaves' lives. The emphasis was on the total control exerted by the system upon the lives of those bound to it. In recent years, however, most studies on slavery have focused on the slaves themselves and on their efforts to develop and maintain a community of "normalcy" for themselves and their families within the limits imposed upon them by their abnormal imprisonment and on their subsequent and successful development of a viable and distinctive Afro-American subculture.

Two authors exemplifying this "new school" of emphasis are Herbert G. Gutman and Eugene D. Genovese. Gutman's, The Black Family In Slavery and Freedom, 1750-1925, (1976), a well researched treatise on slave families, points out a number of factors which affected and characterized the slaves' sense of family. His discussion on the naming patterns of slaves is of special interest to genealogists. Genovese's, Roll Jordan Roll: The World the Slaves Made, (1974), is similar to Gutman's work in that it takes a close personal look at the slaves themselves. Special attention is given to those forces, such as family and religion, which were positive factors in the slaves' lives and enabled them to build an Afro-American "community."

As one progresses with his research and becomes more familiar with his own slave ancestry, it is natural that he will develop an even greater interest in his ancestors' world. To illustrate the wide variety of sources available on slavery, a selected list of references is offered in Appendix D. While these social histories may not help the family historian in his primary goal of identifying his own personal ancestral heritage, they can aid him in the important secondary goal of better understanding that heritage. As family historians, we must never forget that our ancestors lived in a world very different from our own, and we can only hope to understand them as real living beings by placing them, and ourselves, back in that very different world of theirs. The research findings of the genealogist and of the social historian should never be looked upon as exclusive. Important knowledge of mutual interest and benefit can be gained from both foci of investigation.

Historians from many fields of study have come to embrace the idea that historical investigation must encompass all levels of society and have come to appreciate that the history of a society is reflected in the histories of the many individual families within it. The historical evolution of a family over several generations provides the historian with a rare personal glimpse into the historical evolution of the community as a whole. Through the rediscovery of each individual family's heritage, our chances of rediscovering our national heritage are greatly enhanced. In history, as in other disciplines, it is important to remember the old axiom that the whole can be no greater than the sum of its parts. With each new successful journey into our individual families' pasts, we come a little closer to a better understanding and truer portrait of the American people as a whole. No chapter from our past should be forgotten, and no branch of the American "family" should be overlooked. Through the personal struggles of each black American to uncover his or her own ancestral roots, America is better able to more completely discover its own.

The findings presented in this book provide the researcher of slave ancestry with valuable information on how best to approach an investigation of a large section of the slave population which has often been overlooked. Working with the various records found at the county level of government as illustrated in this book, it is possible to identify a number of slave families living in non-plantation settings. These findings not only increase our knowledge of slave families but broaden our perspectives on the conditions of slavery itself.

# CHAPTER I: THE CHALLENGES OF SLAVERY TO THE FAMILY HISTORIAN

The first requirement facing the family historian interested in researching slave ancestors is the need to recognize the special problems involved. Foremost among these difficulties is the fact that since slaves were not considered citizens of the United States, they were not permitted to engage in even the most basic of legal transactions. Even a simple marriage contract between slaves was legally forbidden. Considered by law as part of their owners' property, what traces of the slaves' lives that survive are found scattered among the records of the business transactions of their owners. With no legal status of their own, there are virtually no records concerning slaves which were initiated by the slaves themselves. Unlike the situation for their contemporary white "neighbors," no conscious effort was made to preserve a record of the slaves' lives, and any records which have survived for them are a product of accidental good fortune.

Compounding this already most difficult situation is the further complication that slaves were seldom afforded the distinction of being addressed by a surname. Referred to in records by only a first name, or often listed as just a black male or a black female, the problems of proper identification are enormous and require a much greater amount of corroborating evidence than is generally needed. Studies by scholars such as Gutman and Genovese have shown that among the slaves themselves surnames were fairly common and a valued part of "slave society." These same studies have confirmed that very few whites were aware of this practice, and there was no official recognition of it. While the discovery of the widespread usage of surnames among the slaves is of great significance to social historians, it seldom proves to be of any practical value to the family historian, since the fact remains that the slaves' surnames were either unknown or unaccepted by contemporary whites and do not appear in contemporary records.

Unfortunately, problems with surnames do not end simultaneously with slavery. Once the public usage of surnames became legal, ex-slaves were free either to acknowledge the names they had previously been using in private or to choose a new one. Both of these options proved to be attractive to the former slaves, and it is difficult to discern which was the more common practice. For a variety of reasons (one being the ex-slaves' lingering fears that their emancipation would not be permanent and their corresponding desire to make their recovery as difficult as possible), many ex-slaves continued to change or alter their names for a number of years after their release. An additional obstacle is the predicament where several members of one biological family adopted different last names. This situation, most often found in the years immediately following emancipation, can be explained by a variety of circumstances. Since members of a single slave family often were owned by several different people, slaves when freed sometimes adopted the names of their different owners. In some cases slaves found themselves considerably removed from their family of birth and developed stronger ties with surrogate families in their new surroundings. There is also the case of a slave being sold at an age too young to remember his or her heritage. In some instances an ex-slave mother, for whatever reason, did not adopt the surname used by the father of her children, and the children were confronted with a choice between their parents' names. Whatever the problem concerning the slaves' and ex-slaves' use of surnames may be, it is a dilemma which must be eventually resolved and one unique to slave ancestry.

No one is more aware of the implications that a slave's life was never legally his own than the family historian. With no legal recognition given to slave "marriages" and with no legal protections given to slave families, the same strength, determination and devotion once needed by the slaves to keep their families "together" is now required of the family historian trying to rediscover those families. Severe restrictions were imposed upon the slave families, and the family historian must be aware of those. Sole ownership of all slave children legally resided with the owner of the child's mother, as no legal recognition was given to the father. Although recent studies by social historians such as Gutman and Genovese have shown that slave fathers often played a significant role in their children's lives and in maintaining viable slave "marriages" and families, because no legal recognition was given to them, seldom is any mention made of them in written documents. As a result of this, research work is often limited to the maternal lines.

Another situation sometimes encountered when researching slave ancestors is the possibility of biracial parentage. From a strictly professional perspective this can prove to be a formidable impediment to further research along that particular line. It may also result in complications of a more personal nature, and each individual researcher must evaluate for him- or herself how best to proceed from that point.

The list of difficulties confronting the research of slave ancestry often appears endless, and it is understandable if the task sometimes seems herculean. An especially frustrating problem, affecting virtually all aspects of one's research, is the uncertainty of most slaves' ages. A dramatic description of this is seen in the words of one of America's most famous ex-slaves, Frederick Douglass:

I have no accurate knowledge of my age, never having seen any authentic record containing it. By far the larger part of the slaves know as little of their ages as horses know of theirs, and it is the wish of most masters within my knowledge to keep their slaves thus ignorant. I do not remember to have ever met a slave who could tell of his birthday [6].

One final challenge facing the black family historian should be mentioned. Unfortunately, it is a condition which could have been avoided, since it is a shortcoming found in recently created documents rather than those from the past. Many historical societies and individuals have published great numbers of compilations of data useful to the genealogist such as abstarcts of wills and estate settlements, and indexes of deeds and court records. These publications serve as excellent finding tools and save the researcher incalculable hours of research time. Regrettably, however, many of these publications have failed to include the names of the slaves mentioned in the abstracted documents, and a tedious page-by-page search of the originals is required. While this situation is more of an inconvenience than an obstruction, it is nevertheless a challenge, and one which hopefully will diminish in the future.

## The Preliminary Survey

Genealogical research in the post-slavery period is basically the same for black Americans as it is for whites. Fortunately there are excellent genealogical publications available for this post-slavery period providing helpful instruction to all family historians on general genealogical procedures and techniques. Since this paper deals solely with the problems faced by the family historian in regards to the special question of slavery, only a cursory review of these preliminary basics will be presented here. For a more in-depth study of general genealogical research methods the reader is encouraged to consult the sources listed in the bibliography under the heading of genealogy. The reader should note the listing of several books and articles dealing specifically with black genealogy and become familiar with the particular information each of these has to offer.

Even though there are unique difficulties and challenges confronting the black family historian, there are also a number of organizations, societies and services specifically designed to assist black Americans in the preservation of their special heritage. One of the oldest of these organizations is the Association For the Study of Afro-American Life and History. Located in Washington D.C., it has a membership of over 25,000. One of its projects is the publishing of articles on black history. The Afro-American Historical and Genealogical Society was founded in 1977, with a noted black historian and genealogist, James D. Walker, as its president. Also based in Washington, it publishes its own journal. The Schomburg Center for Research in Black Culture, located in New York City, encourages the preservation of black family histories and serves as a repository for them. R & E Research Associates, Inc., in San Francisco, specialize in publishing books on black American History and on the lives of black Americans. Howard University Library in the nation's capitol is only one of a great number of colleges and universities which house information of special interest to the black historian. In addition, there are many excellent local, state and regional libraries and societies around the country which can provide helpful information and assistance to the family historian interested in a particular locality. While none of these organizations may meet the personal needs of each researcher, especially in the beginning stages of one's research, it is of value to remember that they exist for possible consultation in the future.

In any field of investigation there are basic research fundamentals which

must be adhered to to guarantee accuracy, consistency and the greatest chance of success. Genealogical research is no exception. Whatever the ultimate goal pursued, the first step any family historian must take is to gather and record all known facts. Working from the present to the past, one moves methodically from the known to the unknown carefully recording and properly documenting all information. The best place to begin any genealogical research project is in the home. A family's home is without question the richest repository of that family's history. A search should be made for a wide variety of memorabilia with special attention given to family Bibles, diaries, letters and old photographs. Of even greater importance, the memories of the family members themselves should be thoroughly "searched."

Oral history is one of the family historian's greatest resources, and this is often especially true for black families. A wealth of family history and traditions have been preserved without the benefit of any written documents, and many older relatives can provide the family historian with a bonanza of information. Often the most crucial piece of data needed by the black family historian, the name of the slaves' owner, can be learned from an interview with an older family member. Although few researchers can hope to discover the same exceptionally rich reserve of oral family history as that uncovered by Alex Haley, a wealth of information can be found.

With such a scarcity of written information available on the slaves, and accepting the reality that even for a number of years after the end of slavery this scarcity of written records continued within many black communities, much interest has been generated in programs devoted to the preservation of black oral histories. These programs are attempting to recover as much black history as possible before it is lost forever. In Kentucky, the University of Louisville has been involved in several black oral history projects, and much has been done to save this important segment of the state's past. For further guidance in black oral history, the following articles are recommeneded: Gary Y. Okihiros, "Oral History and the Writing of Ethnic History: A Reconnaissance into Method and Theory," <u>Oral History Review</u> 9 (1980); and George C. Wright's "Oral History and the Search for the Black Past in Kentucky," <u>Oral History Review</u> 10 (1982).

Utilizing conventional genealogical sources and techniques in the post-slavery period, substantial information can be gathered on the families under investigation. Building upon this foundation of data, research can then be extended into the slavery era. Crossing this demarcation necessitates a readjustment of one's work. Traditional record sources and research methods often prove inappropriate or insufficient to meet the peculiar demands of researching slave ancestry. New record sources must be located, traditional sources must be examined in untraditional ways, and novel research goals and techniques must be employed. The best methods for meeting these new research challenges are discussed in detail in the succeeding sections of this study. Special attention is paid to the various types of records found at the county level of government and their significance to the researcher of slave families. A reservoir of primary source material is available at the county level. Work with these records, however, should be preceded by an examination of the information found in the federal censuses. A careful survey of these censuses substantially augments one's data base, and consequently, enhances one's ability to utilize more effectively the county records.

Afro-Americans and Where to Find Them in the Federal Censuses

Since the year 1790, the United States government has conducted a national enumeration of its population at ten-year intervals. These population census schedules are presently available for use by the general public for the years 1790 through 1910. They provide family historians with one of their best overall sources of information. There

are a number of good genealogical guide books which describe in detail the contents and peculiarities of these schedules for each of the census years, and the reader is encouraged to refer to them [7]. The discussions presented in this study are restricted to the relevancy of these records in the researching of slave ancestors.

Following the "golden rule of genealogy" (i.e. working from the known to the unknown), the first targets of investigation are the census schedules for 1910 and 1900. All Americans were listed in these schedules non-discriminatorialy. Every member of a household was named and counted, and the following data was recorded for each person: name, relationship to the head of the household, sex, race, age, month and year of birth, marital status, number of years married, number of children a mother had given birth to and the number of those children still living, place of birth (by state), place of birth of each person's father and mother, and occupation. Additional questions were also asked regarding each family's socio-economic status. With just 35 years separating slavery and the twentieth century, many former slaves were counted in these census schedules, and they serve both to verify information gathered on more immediate family members and to provide clues on the composition of earlier generations.

Questions asked in both the 1910 and 1900 censuses of special interest to the black family historian include: the month and year of birth, place of birth, parents' place of birth, the number of children a mother had given birth to and how many of those children were still living at the time the census was taken. Remembering that very few slave births were officially recorded and recognizing that slave mothers were often separated over the years from some, if not all, of their offspring, the black genealogist often has no clue as to the number of children a slave mother may have had. The 1900 and 1910 censuses provide the researcher with this vital information.

Of great value also are the former slaves' declarations on the number of years they had been married. Although deprived of the sanctions of law, many slaves nevertheless considered their "marriages" valid and binding, and those "marriages" consummated under slavery were acknowledged and honored in freedom and confirmed in the responses of the former slaves to this question in the census.

Unfortunately, the censuses are not arranged in any alphabetical order, and to facilitate locating a family or ancestor in these records one should have a good idea of the family's residence at the time the census was taken. The records are arranged by state, then by county and then by further subdivision within the county itself.

There does exist a semi-alphabetical index, called a Soundex, for the 1900 census. This is a system of indexing by sound rather than by strict alphabetical sequence, and it can serve as a helpful locating tool. The Soundexes are arranged on a statewide basis.

With the 1890 census almost entirely destroyed by fire, the next censuses of interest are the schedules for 1880 and 1870. For the researcher of slave ancestors, census research in a very real sense begins with these years. Between the censuses of 1860 and 1870, Americans fought a bloody Civil War, slavery in America was universally abolished with the ratification of the 13th Amendment, and American society was permanently transformed. The 1870 census reflected this transformation, as for the first time in America's history all Americans, black and white, were listed by name.

The 1870 census records the following data for each American: name, age, sex, color, place of birth, and occupation. Information was asked concerning couples married within the census year, children attending school during the year, the ability of adults to read and write, and the value of real and personal property owned.

Caution is recommended when using the 1870 census to reconstitute family structures. The relationship between the various members listed in a household was not specified in this census, and there are many individuals grouped together in a single household unit who were not related. This is particularly true of households comprising former slaves. Out of necessity many former slaves were forced to unite together for social and economic reasons into quasi-family units. Many of the blacks living together in the 1870 census had lived together earlier as a "family" on their former slaveowners' farms and continued to rely upon these relationships even though there were often no actual kinship ties betwen them.

The 1870 census is significant in that it was often the first official recording of a surname for the former slaves. During their years of bondage few slaves were ever distinguished in written records by the use of a last name. When they received their freedom and became legal citizens, surnames became a privilege and a necessity. A black's surname in the 1870 census can frequently provide the researcher with the best clue as to whom an ex-slave was formerly bonded to, and the researcher has an important lead for beginning the next stage of his research.

Many ex-slaves naturally chose, or were given, the name of a former owner, often the name of their last owner before emancipation. This, however, was not always the case. Some ex-slaves selected the name of a prominent family in the community or of someone of national prominence either living or dead. Others perhaps adopted a name identifying them with a particular skill, trade or characteristic. Historians such as Gutman and Genovese have noted that the newly freed slaves exercised greater diversity and flexibility in the selection of their surnames than previously supposed. It has been suggested that many slaves, rather than choose the name of their most recent owner, went back in time and chose the name of an owner of one of their parents, grandparents or earlier forefathers; some even being able to recall a name associated with their immigrant African ancestor. By establishing such a tie with an early owner, the ex-slaves were actually establishing and preserving an historical link with their own family's past [8]. Whether an ex-slave's name was one taken from a recent owner, from the more distant past, or from some other unrelated source, it is still a valuable clue and a mirror into that slave's past. The researcher must also keep in mind that unlike the situation for many whites, not all blacks in a certain locality or even in a single household who shared a common surname were related. A slave-owner may have "given" his name to a great number of former slaves, and their only ties may have been that name and the bonds of slavery. The census for 1880, although similar to the one in 1870, differed from all preceding schedules in several important aspects. For the first time, not only was the birthplace of each person recorded but also the birthplace of each person's father and mother. The 1880 census was also the first schedule to list the relationship of each member of a household to that household's head. This reduced much of the uncertainty and confusion in the earlier schedules, and it gives the researcher his first real opportunity to convert households into families.

It is important for the family historian to remember when using the censuses that they are products of human labor and as such as are subject to all manner of human error. The wealth of information that they provide cannot be minimized, but they should be approached with caution. Discrepancies in ages given from one census year to another are common for all persons enumerated, and this is especially true of the ages given for blacks in these earlier schedules. Considering what little significance was attached to a slave's exact birth date, the ensuing confusion and uncertainty over ages is understandable. No age given for any one census year should be taken as an absolute truth.

Discrepancies in the censuses are not limited to ages. The researcher will face a variety of differences in the data recorded for the different census years, and common sense will be needed to cope with the variances. One especially troubling inconsistency is in the spelling of names. As this can sometimes make locating a particular family or individual difficult, the researcher should try to anticipate all possible spelling variants.

One discrepancy unique to the re-search of the black family historian concerns the recording of each person's color. Afro-Americans were distinguished in these earlier census schedules according to the color classification, black or mulatto. From a strictly professional point of view, this color distinction provides the researcher with another valuable research tool. The difficulties of properly identifying and distinguishing individual slaves have been mentioned, and the advantage of having as many identifying characteristics as possible is obvious. Where two slaves or ex-slaves are found to have the same name and roughly the same age, the advantage of being able to distinguish betwen them on the basis of their color classification should not be overlooked. Once again however, the researcher is cautioned to avoid accepting the data found in any one census year as the absolute truth. The color classifications for some individuals examined in the schedules for Wayne County have been found to change as often as the censuses themselves, and it must be remembered that all data recorded in the censuses was only as reliable as the knowledge, perspectives and even the prejudices of the individual census takers. Census takers in the 19th century usually were prominent white citizens of a community, and many were not personally acquainted with the county's black residents.

To illustrate some of the possible discrepancies in census data, several examples are given of abstracts taken from the 1870 and 1880 censuses of Wayne County, Kentucky, as shown in Table 1. These abstracts illustrate the range of discrepancies (spelling, age, color, birthplace) that can be found even between two succeeding censuses.

Failure to locate an individual on a census schedule should not be taken as proof that this person was not in the county at that time. A variety of circumstances contribute to a number of people being missed in any particular census year. Thomas R. Ford, Director of the Center for Developmental Change at the Uiversity of Kentucky, concluded after an extensive analysis of the 1880 census, that the white population of Kentucky, in that year was probably 6.5

## TABLE 1

### EXAMPLES OF DATA DISCREPANCIES IN THE CENSUSES

<u>1870</u>                                              <u>1880</u>

Millspring p.17                          Millspring p.8

| | age | color | birth-place | | age | color | relation-ship | birthplace "/Fa/Mo | | |
|---|---|---|---|---|---|---|---|---|---|---|
| Cowan, Ceasar | 56 | Mu | VA | Cow, Sezar | 65 | B | | VA | VA | VA |
| " , Caroline | 39 | Mu | KY | " , Caroline | 43 | B | wife | KY | KY | KY |
| " , Amanda | 15 | Mu | " | | | | | | | |
| " , Beckie | 13 | Mu | " | " , Rebecky | 23 | B | dau. | KY | KY | KY |
| " , Asberry | 12 | Mu | " | " , Asbery | 21 | B | son | " | " | " |
| " , Isaac | 9 | B | " | " , Isac P. | 19 | B | " | " | " | " |
| " , Robert G. | 1 | Mu | " | | | | | | | |
| | | | | " , Magalien | 8 | B | dau. | " | " | " |

------------------------------

Monticello p.32                          Monticello E.D. 106, p.26

| | age | color | birth-place | | age | color | relation-ship | birthplace "/Fa/Mo | | |
|---|---|---|---|---|---|---|---|---|---|---|
| Scott, London | 59 | Mu | VA | Scott, London | 64 | Mu | | VA | VA | VA |
| " , Sarah | 30 | B | KY | " , Sarah | 41 | B | wife | KY | KY | KY |
| " , James | 3 | Mu | " | " , James | 13 | Mu | grandson | " | " | " |

------------------------------

Monticello p.30                          Mullenstown p.6

| | age | color | birth-place | | age | color | relation-ship | birthplace "/Fa/Mo | | |
|---|---|---|---|---|---|---|---|---|---|---|
| Garrett, Abraham | 57 | B | TN | Garret, Abram | 54 | B | | TN | VA | VA |
| " , Kate | 42 | Mu | " | " , Sarah C. | 50 | Mu | wife | TN | - | TN |
| " , Mary A. | 20 | B | " | | | | | | | |
| " , Samuel | 17 | B | KY | | | | | | | |
| " , Andrew | 15 | Mu | TN | | | | | | | |
| " , James | 12 | Mu | KY | | | | | | | |
| " , Margaret | 6 | B | " | " , Margaret J | 16 | Mu | dau. | KY | TN | TN |
| " , Martha | 4 | Mu | " | " , Martha L | 14 | Mu | " | " | " | " |
| " , Henriett | 2 | B | " | " , Henrietta | 12 | B | " | " | " | " |
| " , Isaac B | 1/12 | Mu | " | " , Isaac B | 10 | Mu | son | " | " | " |
| " , Lydia | 75 | Mu | VA | | | | | | | |

SOURCE: 1870 and 1880 U.S. Population Censuses, Wayne County, Kentucky.

percent greater than the census count, and the undercount for the black population was even larger [9]. Considering the disruptions caused by the Civil War, one can safely assume that the imperfections of the census in 1870 were even greater. A study of other Wayne County documents, such as the annual tax lists, shows that there were blacks living in the county who, for whatever reasons, failed to be recorded on the census.

Like the census of 1900, there exists a Soundex for the schedule of 1880. Based on the same semi-alphabetical sound-index system mentioned earlier, this Soundex serves as a helpful guide for the locating of many families in the 1880 census. Unlike the Soundex for 1900, the one for 1880 is not an index of every individual found in the census. It is more limited in that it only includes individuals who were members of a household which included at least one child ten years of age or younger.

One additional thought to keep in mind when working with these records, and in particular when using the schedule for 1870, is the question of neighbors. Once a family has been located in the census, the researcher should then make a note of the families and individuals listed before and after that family on the census sheets. Particular attention should be given to any persons, white and black, sharing the same surname. Especially in 1870, many blacks can be found listed living near their former owners, and this can serve as an additional clue in the important task of identifying the slaveowner.

Prior to the census of 1870, slaves were only enumerated as part of an owner's property. From 1790 through 1860, the records for the slaves were purely statistical, and the slaves' names were not given. Any blacks listed by name in these early general population schedules were free, and all free black Americans should be found in these schedules. Any slave receiving his or her freedom within a given decade should appear on the general population schedule at the beginning of the next decade.

The federal censuses for the years 1850 and 1860 were unique in that they were divided into separate free and slave schedules. All whites and "free-coloreds" were listed in the free schedules with each individual's name, age, sex, color, place of birth and occupation recorded. All slaves were enumerated in the separate slave schedules and were recorded under the name of their owner. These slave schedules like the regular free population schedules were filed by state and by county. The slave schedules of 1850 and 1860 give the name of each slaveowner with a listing of his or her slaves by age, sex and color (black or mulatto). Only slaves over the age of 100 were listed by name. While the information given for slaves is certainly minimal in comparison to that provided in the free schedules, these slave schedules can prove useful. By comparing the ages, sex and color of the slaves with the information given in the later censuses, it is often possible to identify tentatively a slave's owner, and this is the essential first step for any further research into a slave's history.

By comparing the listings of the slaves in the 1850 schedule to those in 1860, one can speculate as to whether a certain slaveowner bought, sold or otherwise acquired or dispensed of any slaves during this ten-year period, and the researcher can better evaluate the probability of finding a record of such a transaction. Special note should be made of any female slaveowners as they may very likely have been widows, alerting the researcher to search for their husbands' estate papers. Likewise, the administrators of an estate still under litigation may be listed as such in the slave schedules as the owners' of that estate's slaves.

The censuses from 1790 through 1840 were strictly statistical in nature for all Americans both free and enslaved, with only free heads of households being named. Slaves were enumerated in these schedules under the name of their owner, and as is the case with the censuses of 1850 and 1860, the principal value of these schedules lies in the identifying of slaveowners. Approximate birthdates of slaves in question can also be determined from the statistics.

In the first census of 1790, only the

# CHART 1

## CENSUS PROFILE OF ALSAY TAYLOR (Slave)

### 1880 Census

E.D. 105 p.3

| | | color | age | relationship | birthplace "/" of father/mother | | |
|---|---|---|---|---|---|---|---|
| #26-26 | Taylor, Joe H. | W | 70 | farmer | KY | KY | TN |
| | " , Levi | W | 101 | boarder | VA | VA | VA |
| | Taylor, Alsay (female) | B | 56 | dom. servant | " | " | " |
| | Copenhaver, Sam | B | 23 | farm laborer | KY | " | -- |
| #23-23 | Taylor, J.H. (male) | B | 23 | farm laborer | KY | KY | VA |
| | " , Mattie | B | 23 | wife | " | " | " |
| | " , Sarah J. | B | 3 | dau. | " | " | KY |
| | " , Robert O. | B | 1 | son | " | " | " |

### 1870 Census

Mill Spring p.30

| | | color | age | occupation | birthplace |
|---|---|---|---|---|---|
| #211 | Taylor, Joseph H. | W | 63 | farmer | KY |
| | " , Alsey (f) | B | 45 | house keeper | VA |
| | " , Susan | B | 19 | | KY |
| | " , James | B | 12 | farm laborer | " |
| | " , Lucy | B | 10 | | " |

### 1860 Slave Schedule

| owner | slaves: | age / | sex / | color | # of slave houses |
|---|---|---|---|---|---|
| Joseph Taylor | | 35 | f | B | 1 |
| | | 10 | f | B | |
| | | 2 | M | B | |
| | | 1 | f | B | |

### 1850 Slave Schedule

| owner | slaves: | age / | sex / | color |
|---|---|---|---|---|
| Levi T. Taylor | | 24 | f | B |
| | | 4 | f | B |
| | | 2 | f | B |

13

# CHART 2

## CENSUS PROFILE OF JOSHUA COIL (Slave)

### 1900 Census

E.D. 128 p.10

| | | color | age | month & yr of birth | | birthplace "/father/mother | | | |
|---|---|---|---|---|---|---|---|---|---|
| #174-178 | Coil, Joshua | B | 80 | Jan 1820 | | MD | MD | MD | married 31 years |
| " | , Clerissa | B | 60 | Aug 1839 | wife | TN | - | GA | 8 child - 5 alive |
| " | , Matilda | B | 29 | Jul 1870 | dau. | KY | MD | TN | single |
| " | , James R. | B | 28 | Nov 1871 | son | " | " | " | " |
| " | , Wm. | B | 26 | Aug 1873 | " | " | " | " | " |
| " | , Jermiah | B | 23 | Apr 1877 | " | " | " | " | " |
| " | , Samuel | B | 15 | Oct 1884 | " | " | " | " | " |

### 1880 Census

Slickford p.24

| | | color | age | relationship | birthplace "/father/mother | | |
|---|---|---|---|---|---|---|---|
| #220-222 | Coil, Josh | B | 60 | farmer | VA | VA | VA |
| " | , Clerry | B | 40 | wife | KY | -- | -- |
| " | , Matilda | B | 10 | dau. | KY | VA | KY |
| " | , James | B | 8 | son | " | " | " |
| " | , William | B | 6 | " | " | " | " |
| " | , Jerry | B | 4 | " | " | " | " |
| " | , Amos | B | 1 | " | " | " | " |

### 1870 Census

Slickford p.16

| | | color | age | occupation | birthplace |
|---|---|---|---|---|---|
| #113-113 | Coil, Joshua | B | 50 | farmer | VA |
| " | , Clarissa | B | 30 | | KY |
| " | , Henry | B | 9 | | " |
| Dalton, Milly | | B | 50 | | GA |
| " | , Robert | B | 15 | | KY |

### 1860 Slave Schedule

| owner | slaves: age / sex / color | | | # of slave houses |
|---|---|---|---|---|
| James Coyle | 40 | m | B | 1 |

### 1850 Slave Schedule

| owner | slaves: age / sex / color | | |
|---|---|---|---|
| James Coyle | 30 | m | B |

total number of slaves was recorded with no distinction made as to sex. There were no separate free and slave schedules, and the number of slaves owned by each head of household was given after the statistics for the free members of that household. The censuses of 1800 and 1810 remained virtually the same for the enumeration of slaves.

In 1820, slaves were divided by sex and then enumerated under the following four age groups: under 14; 14 and under 26; 26 and under 45; 45 and older. These age categories were also used for "free coloreds." Unless a free black was the head of his own household, his name was not given.

The censuses of 1830 and 1840, again statistical in nature, gave the slave and free colored enumerations on a slightly broader age distribution: under 10; 10 and under 24; 24 and under 36; 36 and under 55; 55 and under 100; 100 and upwards. Again males and females were counted separately. Special count was also taken of all coloreds who were either deaf and dumb or blind. These enumerations of the slaves are found on the page following the enumerations of their owners.

The following are abstracts of the data found in the federal censuses for Wayne County [10]. They are offered as examples of the process of tracking an individual or family through the census schedules, and illustrate some of the opportunities and limitations involved in census research. Through the information gathered from this record group, other avenues of investigation become visible. (See Chart 1.) Joseph Taylor was not listed as a slaveowner in the 1850 Schedule, and Levi Taylor was not listed as an owner in 1860. It appears that Alsay (Aelsey) Taylor who was a domestic servant for Joseph H. Taylor in 1870 and 1880, was the same 35-year-old female slave owned by Joseph Taylor in 1860, and the 24-year-old female slave owned by Levi T. Taylor in 1850.

J. H. Taylor, the 23-year-old black farmer living near Joseph and Levi Taylor in the 1880 Census, was very likely the 12-year-old James Taylor living in the household of Joseph Taylor in 1870. He was probably the same 2-year-old male slave owned by Joseph Taylor in 1860, and it would be practical to pursue the idea that Alsay was his mother. Although this cannot be proven based solely on the data given for these census years, the researcher is provided with a number of theories and information worthy of further investigation. (See Chart 2.)

The 30-year-old male slave owned in 1850 by James Coyle would appear to be the same Joshua Coil who was 80 years old in 1900. It is not possible from the census data alone to determine unequivocally that this was so, but the censuses show that it would be wise to check other records pertaining to James Coyle for any mention of his slave. Undoubtedly, a number of perplexing discrepancies will be encountered in the censuses, and common sense is needed to unravel these differences. It is not difficult to imagine Coil and Coyle being spelling variants of the same name, and a more extensive survey of additional records proves this to be so.

Although the censuses do not give the maiden name of Joshua Coil's wife Clerissa, they provide the perceptive researcher with a clue. Clerissa Coil answered in 1900, that her mother was born in Georgia. Milly Dalton, who was living with the Joshua Coil family in 1870, was also born in Georgia, and she was of a feasible age to have been Clerissa's mother. This is another avenue of investigation that the researcher will want to follow. (See Chart 3.)

While the censuses alone do not verify that Charles Sandusky was once a slave of Emanuel Sandusky, a number of elements seem to indicate that this was so and confirm the feasibility of further research into Emanuel Sandusky's records for any mention of Charles and his family. Al-though one must consider the possiblility of Charles having been owned by someone other than a member of the Sandusky family, it is always wiser to investigate the more obvious possibilities first.

There were only two owners listed in the 1860 and 1850 slave schedules by the name of Sandusky, Emanuel and Jacob. When a comparison is made of the data

# CHART 3

## CENSUS PROFILE OF CHARLES SANDUSKY (Slave)

### 1900 Census

E.D. 126 p.5

| | | color | month & yr of birth | | birthplace "/father/mother | | | |
|---|---|---|---|---|---|---|---|---|
| #6-6 | Sandusky, Wm. R. | B | Mar 1863 | | KY KY KY | | | married 16 yrs |
| " | , Jane | B | May 1870 | wife | " " " | | | 5 child-3 alive |
| " | , Love | B | Jun 1885 | dau. | " " " | | | |
| " | , Mary | B | Sep 1892 | " | " " " | | | |
| " | , Minnie | B | Apr 1895 | " | " " " | | | |
| | | | | | | | | |
| #7-7 | Sandusky, Granvil M. | B | Mar 1869 | | KY KY KY | | | married 7 yrs |
| " | , Laura B. | B | Aug 1878 | wife | " " " | | | 4 child-4 alive |
| " | , Will L. | B | Feb 1894 | son | " " " | | | |
| " | , Dora B. | B | Aug 1895 | dau. | " " " | | | |
| " | , Mamie T. | B | Oct 1896 | " | " " " | | | |
| " | , Lizzie E. | B | Jan 1899 | " | " " " | | | |
| | | | | | | | | |
| #8-8 | Sandusky, Colonel L. | B | Jul 1872 | | KY KY KY | | | married 10 yrs |
| " | , Maggie | B | Aug 1875 | wife | " " " | | | 1 child-1 alive |
| " | , Elmer | B | Apr 1891 | son | " " " | | | |
| | | | | | | | | |
| #9-9 | Sandusky, Charles | B | Apr 1835 | | KY KY SC | | | married 43 yrs |
| " | , Nancy E. | B | Oct 1839 | wife | " SC VA | | | 14 child-9 alive |
| " | , Lucy E. | B | Nov 1881 | dau. | " KY KY | | | |
| " | , Walter E. | B | Apr 1884 | son | " " " | | | |
| | | | | | | | | |
| #14-14 | Sandusky, General S. | B | Feb 1866 | | KY KY KY | | | married 4 yrs |
| " | , Tilda | B | Nov 1869 | wife | " " " | | | no children |

### 1880 Census

Southfork p.5

| | | color | age | relationship | birthplace "/father/mother | | |
|---|---|---|---|---|---|---|---|
| #48-49 | Sandusky, Charley | Mu | 50 | farmer | KY KY KY | | |
| " | , Nancy E. | B | 45 | wife | " " " | | |
| " | , William R. | Mu | 18 | son | " " " | | |
| " | , Elizabeth | Mu | 15 | dau. | " " " | | |
| " | , General S. | Mu | 12 | son | " " " | | |
| " | , Martha T. | Mu | 10 | dau. | " " " | | |
| " | , Granville | Mu | 8 | son | " " " | | |
| " | , Littleton C. | Mu | 6 | " | " " " | | |
| " | , L.J. (female) | Mu | 9/12 | dau. | " " " | | |

16

# CHART 3

## (continued)

### 1870 Census

Parmsleyville Dist. 4 (Southfork) p.13

|        |                      | color | age  | occupation | birthplace |
|--------|----------------------|-------|------|------------|------------|
| #90-90 | Sandusky, Charles    | Mu    | 35   | farmer     | KY         |
|        | " , Mary E.          | B     | 25   |            | "          |
|        | " , Rebecca          | B     | 15   |            | "          |
|        | " , Emily            | Mu    | 10   |            | "          |
|        | " , William          | Mu    | 8    |            | "          |
|        | " , Elizabeth        | Mu    | 6    |            | "          |
|        | " , Sherrod (m)      | Mu    | 4    |            | "          |
|        | " , Martha           | Mu    | 2    |            | "          |
|        | " , Granville        | Mu    | 4/12 |            | "          |

### 1860 Slave Schedule

| owner:           | slaves: age/sex/color |   |              | owner:          | slaves: age/sex/color |   |   |
|------------------|-----|---|--------------|-----------------|----|---|---|
| Emanuel Sandusky | 53  | f | B            | Jacob Sandusky  | 24 | f | B |
|                  | 30  | m | B            |                 | 9  | f | B |
|                  | 27  | f | B            |                 | 5  | f | B |
|                  | 25  | m | Mu (Charles) |                 | 3  | m | B |
|                  | 22  | m | B            |                 | 1  | f | B |
|                  | 21  | f | B            |                 |    |   |   |
|                  | 17  | f | B            |                 |    |   |   |
|                  | 14  | m | B            |                 |    |   |   |
|                  | 11  | m | B            |                 |    |   |   |
|                  | 10  | m | Mu           |                 |    |   |   |
|                  | 5   | m | B            |                 |    |   |   |

### 1850 Slave Schedule

| owner:           | slaves: age/sex/color |   |              | owner:         | slaves: age/sex/color |   |   |
|------------------|-----|---|--------------|----------------|----|---|---|
| Emanuel Sandusky | 45  | f | Mu           | Jacob Sandusky | 17 | f | B |
|                  | 24  | f | B            |                |    |   |   |
|                  | 22  | m | B            |                |    |   |   |
|                  | 20  | f | B            |                |    |   |   |
|                  | 16  | m | Mu (Charles) |                |    |   |   |
|                  | 14  | m | B            |                |    |   |   |
|                  | 12  | f | B            |                |    |   |   |
|                  | 10  | f | B            |                |    |   |   |
|                  | 7   | f | B            |                |    |   |   |
|                  | 5   | m | B            |                |    |   |   |
|                  | 2   | m | B            |                |    |   |   |
|                  | 1   | m | B            |                |    |   |   |

CHART 3

(continued)

1840 Census

p.172

Emanuel Sandusky - the listings for his slaves are given in the general census
after the listings for the white members of his household.

male slaves:   2   under 10 years old        female slaves:  1   under 10
               1   10 and under 24                           1   10 and under 24
                                                             1   24 and under 36

1830 Census

p.244

Emanuel Sandusky - listings for his slaves

            males   2   under 10              females:  1  under 10
                    1   24 and under 36                 2  24 and under 36
                    1   46 and under 55

given for their respective slaves with the data given in the later censuses for Charles, such a comparison reveals that Charles could not have been one of the slaves listed for Jacob, but a credible match can be made with the data given for the slaves owned by Emanuel Sandusky. It is conceivable that Charles could well have been one of the two male slaves under the age of 10 owned by Emanuel Sandusky in 1840. Likewise, one of the female slaves between the ages of 24 and 35 owned by Emanuel in 1830 could feasibly have been Charles' mother. Additional information is needed to confirm these possibilities, but the censuses provide valuable clues on the most practical direction for future research to follow.

Charles Sandusky's wife was recorded as Mary E. in 1870, and as Nancy E. in 1880 and 1900. This could be just another example of the wide discrepancies found in the censuses or they could have been two distinct individuals. Noting that Charles in the 1900 census said he had been married 43 years, it seems likely that "Mary" and "Nancy" were the same woman. Mrs. Charles Sandusky answered in 1900 that she had given birth to fourteen children and that nine of these children were still living. Using only the information given in the censuses, we know the names of nine of these children, and can speculate safely on the names of two more, Rebecca and Emily, listed in 1870.

As these examples have demonstrated, working with the censuses is the logical first step in bridging slavery and post-slavery research. Building upon the data extracted from these federal records, research of other record sources becomes possible. With the censuses serving as a guide, one's research next focuses on the information found in records produced at the county level, as discussed in the next chapter.

## CHAPTER II: UTILIZING COUNTY RECORDS

Life in America until roughly the beginning of the twentieth century, and certainly during the years of slavery, was local rather than national in scope. In a world not yet altered by modern technology, it was the county which most often represented the unit of greatest legal and social importance for the vast majority of Americans. Their lives were played out within the borders of this local community, and as a consequence, the county became the repository of much of America's history. Reflecting this earlier importance of the county government, most records of significance for the family historian prior to 1900 are found at the county level.

To facilitate a more detailed examination of the potential usages of these county records, the discussions presented in this study have been deliberately restricted to the records of one county. The records examined for Wayne County, Kentucky are similar to county records found throughout the slave states and have been chosen to illustrate the types of resources available.

Wayne County is situated in central Kentucky along the Tennessee-Kentucky border. Its early settlers who came to the region at the end of the eighteenth century were principally a mixture of pioneers from Virginia, the Carolinas, Georgia and neighboring Tennessee. The vast majority of its citizens came from slave-owning territories, and its social and political institutions were a reflection of that southern heritage. A rural agricultural community, the small family farm was the norm. The county was officially incorporated in 1801, and its records begin that year [11].

A slave territory from the beginning, a racial profile of the county through-out the nineteenth century is presented in Table 2. Using data from the 1850 slave schedule, Table 3 shows the breakdown of the number of slaves per owner. There were 830 slaves recorded on the 1850 schedule divided among 191 owners, for an average of 4.3 slaves per owner. With well over half of the slaves living in groups of four or less, the probability of several members of a single slave family being divided among several owners seems likely. This situation, contrasting sharply with the conditions of slave families on plantations, is significant. When working with the county's records, the assumption cannot be made that the slaves owned by a single owner constituted a complete family unit.

Five principal types of county records pertinent to genealogical research are presented in this chapter. Each record group is identified, and its importance to the study of slave ancestry is discussed. These five record groups, vital records, probates, deeds, court orders, and tax lists, constitute the bulk of the information available on non-plantation slave families.

### Vital Records: How Available Are They?

. Birth, death and marriage records when available are naturally the most valuable source of primary data. Unfortunately, the United States has had no program of national registration of vital statistics, and registration by most state governments was not required until the beginning of the twentieth century. In Kentucky, state sponsored registration did not begin until 1911. For several short periods during the

TABLE 2

WAYNE COUNTY, KENTUCKY'S WHITE AND BLACK POPULATIONS
IN THE 19TH CENTUTRY

| Year | White | Slave | Free Colored |
|------|-------|-------|--------------|
| 1810 | 5,200 | 230 | - |
| 1820 | 7,393 | 553 | 5 |
| 1830 | 8,046 | 633 | 6 |
| 1840 | 6,754 | 630 | 15 |
| 1850 | 7,855 | 830 | 7 |
| 1860 | 9,244 | 987 | 28 |
| 1870 | 9,927 | - | 675 |
| 1880 | 11,613 | - | 899 |
| 1890 | 12,234 | - | 618 |

SOURCE: Ninth Census of the United States,
1870: Population and Social Statistics (Washington: Government Printing Office, 1894); and
Compendium of the Eleventh Census 1890, Part II
(Washington: Government Printing Office, 1894).


TABLE 3

DISTRIBUTION OF SLAVES AMONG OWNERS IN WAYNE COUNTY IN 1850

| # of Slaves | # of Owners | % of Owners |
|-------------|-------------|-------------|
| 1 | 49 | 25.7 |
| 1-4 | 120 | 62.8 |
| 5-9 | 47 | 24.6 |
| 10-15 | 20 | 10.5 |
| 16-20 | 3 | 1.6 |
| over 20 | 1 | 0.5 |

# The owner with the most slaves in 1850
was Alex Daugherty with 22.

SOURCE: 1850 U.S. Slave Schedule Census,
Wayne County, Kentucky.

22

mid-1800's, Kentucky encouraged the registration of births and deaths on a county basis. The resulting records have been preserved for a number of Kentucky's counties for the years from 1852-1859, and again from 1874-1878. These nineteenth century birth and death records have been collected by the Kentucky Historical Society and can be found at the Society's library in Frankfort. They also have been microfilmed by the Genealogical Society of the LDS Church and are available at their library in Salt Lake City or through loan to one of their branch libraries around the country.

Birth and death records have been preserved for Wayne County for the years 1852-1859, 1874 and 1878. These records include the births and deaths of a great number of slaves and are an invaluable source of information. Most of the entries for slave births give the date of birth, the slave's sex, color (black or mulatto), the name of the slave's owner, and, frequently, the given name of the slave. While not always the case, the name of the slave's mother may also be found. Unlike the contemporary birth records for Wayne County's white residents, no records have been found giving the name of the slave's father. Those death records available for slaves usually give the slave's name, age at death, cause of death, place of birth, and the name of the slave's owner.

When working with these records one must remember that not all slave births and deaths were recorded as no strict enforcement of registration existed. For those slaves that were listed, these vital records are the logical first step of investigation after the censuses. When used in conjunction with the data provided in the censuses, they can help confirm, expand and extend the slave's pedigree.

Another potential source of information regarding the deaths of some slaves are the federal mortality schedules taken in conjunction with the general population census schedules for the years 1850 through 1880. These mortality schedules list the deaths of all persons who died within one of these census years, for example between June 1879 and June 1880, with the 1850 and 1860 mortality schedules including the deaths of slaves. These records give the deceased's name, age at death, sex, color, birthplace, cause of death, the month in which the death occurred, and whether the deceased was a slave or free. Theoretically, all slaves who died between June 1849 and June 1850, or June 1859 and June 1860, should be listed in these schedules.

Marriage records have traditionally been kept in America on a county basis and are available for white Americans since the earliest days of a county's formation. Marriage records for most black Americans, however, are not available until after their emancipation. Registration of marriages for blacks legally should have begun no later than 1868 with the adoption of the 14th Amendment, but this was not always the case. Because registration of black marriages continued to be scant and sporadic in a number of localities long after the ex-slaves became legal citizens, the records of each county need to be examined on an individual basis. In some instances separate registers may have been kept for a county's white and black citizens. This possibility should be investigated. The researcher will especially want to investigate any marriages recorded in the first post-emancipation decade, as these marriage registers may contain the only written record of a maiden name for former female slaves.

## How to Effectively Approach Probate Records

One of the great ironies of researching slave ancestry is the fact that one of the most valuable sources of information available is provided by the slave-owners themselves. These are of course the owners' Last Will and Testaments. Probate records serve as one of the principal cornerstones for the building of any genealogical pedigree, and this maxim applies to black genealogy as well, albeit in a roundabout way.

Whenever an individual dies in possession of property, state laws require that the property be distributed or disposed of in a legal manner. If the deceased dies having left a will, he is said to have died testate. The testate estate in due course is distributed according to the personal dictates expressed in the will, and the executor, named by the deceased to manage the settlement of the estate, is given legal authority by the local court to carry out the terms of the will.

Whenever a person dies having failed to leave a will, he is said to have died intestate. The property left in an intestate estate is then distributed according to the laws of inheritance of the appropriate state of jurisdiction. Since no executor is named to manage the estate's settlement, an administrator is duly appointed by the court to fulfill those duties. One of the first tasks required of the administrator is the taking of a complete itemized inventory and appraisal of all real and personal property owned by the deceased at the time of death. The law requires that the inventory and appraisal be legally recorded in the county records, and they can serve as a vital source of information for the family historian. The administrator of an intestate estate is also required to record any bills of sale of the deceased's property and is obligated to submit a record of the final distribution of the estate's holdings. Since slaves were legally considered property, they figure prominently in the probate records of slaveowners.

Probate records are kept on a county basis. Most counties have filed their probate records in separate court books, and many of the early wills and estate inventories have been indexed. Once a possible slaveowner has been identified through the census or other records, a search should be made to locate the owner's will. If the owner died intestate and no will is available, the probate records should still be searched for an inventory, appraisal and record of distribution of the estate. Experience in working with early county records has shown that many records were seemingly "misfiled" and can be found in any of a number of county and court registers. Estate settlements have been found in Court Order Books as well as in Deed Books, and no source should be overlooked when searching for the elusive document.

The potential value of probate records to the researcher of slave ancestors can best be illustrated by giving several actual examples. By reading through the several wills and inventories given in the appendices, the reader should be able to appreciate the wealth of information they offer. Often familial relationships between slaves are given in a will which cannot be determined from any other source. Wills not only tell us when a slave passed from one owner to another but also reveal the new owner's identity. Although the estate inventories occasionally give a slave's age, even when this is not the case the slave's appraised market value can usually be used to at least determine whether the slave was a child or an adult. By working with the probate records of a slaveowning family through several generations, the researcher is often able to also trace several generations of slaves.

### County Deed Books: The Black Genealogist's Best Friend

Perhaps the richest repositories of primary data concerning slaves are the county deed books. Since slaves were legally considered property, it was necessary to officially record any actions affecting the ownership of a slave, and these transactions were usually recorded in a county's deed books. A wide variety of information can be found entered in these books, and they are often not only the best source for solving a difficult genealogical problem but frequently the only one.

As is the case with almost all records relating to the years of slavery, the key to researching deed books lies in researching the records of the various slaveowners. If the name of a slave's owner can be determined, or at least tentatively identified, by the use of census, probate or vital records as discussed earlier, then a systematic search can be undertaken in the deed books for all entries relating to that owner and his family. Since slaves were mentioned in a wide assortment of documents, all entries should be examined. Those records of principal interest are: bills of sale, deeds of gift, hirings, mortgages, records of importation, and manumissions.

The most familiar deed relating to slaves is the bill of sale. Whenever a slave was sold by one owner to another, the transaction was recorded in the deed books. Although there was no set format for the recording of this information, almost all bills of sale provide certain basic and essential data. Bills of sale give the name of the buyer, the name of the seller, their respective counties of residence, the date of the sale, the market value of the slave, and often the slave's name, age and sex. As is the case in working with estate inventories, even when the age of a slave is not given, the slave's market value can at least be used to help determine whether the slave was a child or an adult. By researching the deed books for these bills of sale, one is able to trace the transference of a slave through a series of owners. Because the residence of both the buyer and the seller is given, these deeds provide essential information on the slave's places of residence as well. A good example of this is a bill of sale found in Wayne County's Deed Book A, p.118. The transaction in question took place in 1804, and the accompanying bill of sale shows that Anthony Gholson of Wayne County, Kentucky bought a 26-year-old male slave named Cambridge for $450.00 from William Neelly of Claiborne County, Mississippi [12].

The frequency of slave sales and the percentage of the slave population affected by these sales are questions which have been debated since the earliest days of slavery. Once a controversy having an intense emotional impact on both national politics and the national psyche, the debate over the actual number of slaves sold and the impact these sales had on the lives of those slaves, their families and friends continues to be a source of intense discussion and disagreement. Naturally, the issues raised by this ongoing debate have special interest to anyone concerned with slave families. Herbert G. Gutman's, Slavery and the Numbers Game: A Critique of 'Time on the Cross', (1975), presents an able discourse on the various aspects of this question.

As one begins to review the various bills of sale recorded in a county's deed books, one notices that most sales involved individual slaves. One cannot help but speculate on the impact these sales must have had on the slaves' families. The following quotes illustrate the diversity of opinions that have been offered over the years on this particular aspect of the issue. Ivan E. McDougle, Slavery In Kentucky (1918), "Most slaveowners took care that the family relationships of the slaves should not be disturbed." [13] Clarence L. Mohr, "Slavery in Oglethorpe County, Georgia," Phylon, (1972), "Available evidence indicates that most Oglethorpe [Georgia] blacks were bought and sold on a purely pragmatic basis, with little or no regard for family ties." [14] It would appear that regardless of its outcome the sale of a slave resulted from one of five general causes.

1. The settlement of an estate.
2. The financial difficulties of an owner.
3. The avariciousness of slave traders.
4. The sale of unclaimed captured runaways.
5. The unmanageability of a slave.

Those sales resulting from the proper distribution of an estate's property have been noted earlier. Charles Sydnor in his book on slavery in Mississippi emphasized the second of these causes, "Enormous numbers of negroes were sold by sheriffs and trustees to satisfy debts, particularly in periods of business depression, such as the panic of 1837." [15] Whichever one of these causes, or a combination of them, triggered the sale of a slave, the underlying factor of importance for the family historian is the resulting transference of the slave's ownership.

Not all transferences of slaves from one owner to another were through sales. A great number of slaves were transferred from one owner to a new one by deeds of gift. Owners who would not consider selling their slaves on the open market, would not hesitate to give a slave to one of their children as a gift: as a wedding present, as an investment, as a means to help a child set up their own housekeeping or as a departing gift when a child moved away. Although no actual sale of property was involved, a legal transference of property did occur, and an official recording of this transaction was required by law. Deeds of gift contain the same valuable clues and information. Deed Book B, p.108-109, records two deeds of gift for Anthony Gholson in 1813. In the first of these, Gholson gave to his daughter Nancy, a 20-year-old male slave named Bazel, and a 20-year-old female slave named Rose. In the second deed of gift, Anthony Gholson gave to his granddaughter, Harriet Gholson, a 3-year-old slave girl named Rhoda [16].

Another important transaction affecting the ownership of a slave, at least on a temporary basis, was the hiring out of a slave for a specific length of time or a specific job. This was an important aspect of slavery, but one that is often overlooked. As Frederic Bancroft, a specialist on slave trading, noted, "When slave property was in probate, or possessed by a life-tenant unable to employ it, or belonged to orphan children or other wards in chancery, it was usually necessary to hire out the slaves. Hirings might be made publicly or privately, at almost any time or place and for any period." [17] In Deed Book A, p.106 there is a recording of a power of attorney given by Mary M. Hopky on August 15, 1804, to Edward N. Cullom, both of Wayne County. Mary Hopky had empowered Cullom to act on her behalf to sue a Mr. William J. Sallie of Pulaski County, Kemtucky, for the return of one of her slaves. Mary Hopky had hired out her slave boy Harry to work for Mr. Sallie the previous winter, and he had failed to return the slave to her [18]. In 1836, several of the slaves belonging to the estate of Ambrose Weaver were

hired out for short durations of time before a final settlement of the estate was made and the slaves were sold to their new owners [19]. The essential features comprising most hiring contracts included: some identification of the slave being hired, the length of time the contract was to be in force or an explanation of some particular task to be accomplished by the slave, and the negotiated price.

Since slaves were treated as property, they were often used as security for loans. These mortgages involving slaves as collateral were recorded in the county's deed books. The information contained in these documents varies considerably, but all such mortgage deeds provide important information relating to the life of the slave. From these mortgages one can learn when and why a slave disappears from a certain owner's household. The researcher must consider the possibility that the conditions of the mortgage were unable to be met, and the search for documents relating to a particular slave would then need to shift to the new owner. While these deeds do not always give the mortgaged slave's name, the slave's age and sex were almost always recorded. A deed found on p.133 of Deed Book A, shows that William Beard mortgaged an 8-year-old negro boy in 1805, to Christopher Catrine for a specific sum of money. The deed specifies that Beard had 3 months to repay the loan to regain title of the slave [20]. A deed found on p.415 of Deed Book D, reveals that John Shoemate had three slaves returned to him which he had earlier mortgaged to Robert M. Smith [21].

It is essential when attempting to trace slave ancestors that one become familiar with the laws of each pertinent state or territory regarding the institution of slavery. Without such a survey of the laws, valuable information can often be overlooked. Kentucky, for example, passed several laws pertaining to the importation of slaves into the state, and a knowledge of these laws can alert the researcher to more obscure sources of information. From the beginning Kentucky aligned itself as a slave state. The Kentucky Legislature adopted the state's first slave laws in 1794, and with some minor revisions and clarifications in 1798, 1814 and 1815, these laws remained the basis of Kentucky's legal controls over the institution of slavery until its end in 1865. Although Kentucky legally sanctioned slavery, there existed within the state strong sentiment opposed to the more unpleasant avaricious practice of slave trading. To discourage such activity and at the same time insure the rights of "legitimate" slaveowners, the state passed laws forbidding the importation of slaves as merchandise but guaranteeing every citizen the right to import slaves for their own personal use. Once the slaves were within the state's boundaries there was no penalty for reselling them, and there were many violations of the spirit, if not the letter, of the law. A sizable portion of Kentucky's citizens vocalized their continued opposition to the trafficing in slaves, and in 1833, the legislature passed a law prohibiting all future importation of slaves even for personal use. The only exceptions to this were emigrants coming to the state who were allowed to bring their slaves with them, if they took the oath called for in the Law of 1815: "I _____ do swear that my removal to the state of Kentucky was with the intention of becoming a citizen thereof, and that I have brought no slave or slaves to this state, with the intention of selling them." [22] Many of the state's resident slaveowners opposed this new restriction, and the law was repealed in 1849. The situation reverted to pre-1833 status, permitting any citizen to once again bring slaves into the state for personal use.

As early as 1794, Kentucky required that all slaves brought across its borders had to be registered by their owners with the local authorities. Owners were required to testify that they had brought the slaves into the state for their own use. Deed Book D, p.314, contains the following entry:

I do certify that Rolen Burnet came this day before me Ransom Vanwinkle a Justice of the peace for Wayne County Kentucky and made oath that he had brought five negroes to the state of Kentucky for his own service and that he did not bring them with the intention of selling them and their names is Sivey Stephen Stephen David and Mary, Given under my hand this 22nd Day of February 1827, Ranson Vanwinkle [23].

Using these records of importation the researcher can learn when a slave first arrived at a certain locality and the identity of the owner who brought the slave into the state. Many of these records also frequently reveal where a slave had resided earlier. Ivan E. McDougle's, Slavery in Kentucky, (1918, reprint 1970), provides an excellent summary of that state's slavery laws. There are comparable works available for each of the slave states, some of which are noted in the selected references on slavery found in Appendix D.

The last category of deeds under consideration are manumission records. These are official certificates of freedom. While they appear all too seldom in the deed books, those records which can be found have great genealogical, historical and personal value. When a slave for whatever reason was given his or her freedom, an official record was made of this action. A certificate of freedom was given to the freed slave, and an official recording was entered into a local registry, usually the county's deed books. Subsequent to a law passed in 1823, all manumission records were required to be accompanied by a physical description of the freed slave [24]. On March 24, 1851, the Kentucky Legislature passed an act preventing negroes given their freedom in Kentucky after that date to remain within the state. An act was passed in March 1860, extending this prohibition to all free negro immigration into the state [25]. From the several manumissions found in the deed books of Wayne Couty, a variety of information was obtained. Along with the freed slave's name and age, the terms if any of the slave's freedom and the feelings and motives of the owner were given.

A county's deed books contain a wide assortment of records other than the six principal documents mentioned here. Many deed books have been indexed facilitating a search of their records, but the slaves themselves will seldom be named in these indices. Examples of the principal types of deeds discussed here can be found in the appendices.

## Treasure Hunting in the Court Order Books

The county court order books, like the deed books mentioned earlier, can prove to be a storehouse of valuable and varied information for the researcher of slave ancestry. The court order books are the official recordings of all actions taken by or brought before the county court. A wide range of documents can be found in these books, and a diligent investigation of the court records will reward the researcher with an interesting array of information to supplement and complement findings from other sources. Like other records relating to the period of slavery, the court records in most cases should be approached from the perspective of the slaveowner. Whereas a majority of the deed books have been indexed, the situation for the court order books is not as favorable. It is often necessary to check these books on a page-by-page basis. While tedious and time consuming work, the rewards from such a search are potentially so promising that the researcher is strongly encouraged not to ignore this valuable source of information. As an illustration of the various types of records and data found within the pages of the court order books, several examples abstracted from the court order books of Wayne County are given below.

Court Order Book A, p. 32 [26]:

Ephraim Guffee Jr. and his negro man Sam are exempted from the payment of County levies in future on account of age and infirmity, 1802.

This entry identifies both an owner and a slave who would not have been found in subsequent tax lists and who could have possibly died before the next census. Without this data from the court book, the researcher might not have known that Ephraim Guffee was a slaveowner and would not have known to check other record sources for mention of his slave(s).

Court Order Book G, p. 30 [27]:

On motion of Matilda Gibson Ordered that her infant son Richard colored boy aged eight years on the 6th day of July 1858 be bound an apprentice to Samuel Hensley until he arrives to 21 years of age to be bound and instructed in the art of farming and that Clerk of this Court execute with Said Hensley the appropriate Indenture of Apprenticeship which was accordingly done and acknowledged in open Court by Said Clerk & Hensley. July Term 1858.

This record served to identify the mother of Richard Gibson, a mulatto boy found in the 1860 free census listed as living in the household of a white man, Samuel Hensly.

Court Order Book G, p.74 [28]:

March 1st 1859 Satisfactory reasons appearing to the Court from the evidence of Martin Coyle It is ordered that Moses Phillips a free boy of color aged about four years be bound an apprentice unto the Said Martin Coyle until he arrives at 21 years of age to be taught and instructed the art of farming - and that the said Martin Coyle execute with the Clerk of the Court the appropriate Indenture of Apprenticeship.

Since the young boy Moses Phillips was both "colored" and free and since no manumission record was found for him, it is logical to assume that he was born free. For this to have been the case there are two possibilities. First, he could have been the son of a black woman who was free at the time of his birth which would have made him free as well;

or he could have been the son of a white woman and a black father. Since legally the state of being born either free or a slave was solely dependent upon the status of a child's mother, the status of the child's father had no bearing whatsoever on the legal status of the child.

Court Order Book D, p.35 [29]:

At a County Court began and held for Wayne County at the courthouse in the town of Monticello on the 4th Monday being the 28th day of January 1839...
The last Will and testament of George Ewing deceased was this day produced to the Court and proven in Open Court...
Simon (commonly called Si) and Juda, his wife, two negroes who were emancipated by the last will and Testament of the said George Ewing being called this day came into Court - and in pursuance to the Act of Assembly in such cases made & provided a description of of said Negroes was, by order, taken and is as follows, towit: -
Simon (commonly called Si) is about 57 years old, 5 feet 9 inches & a half high, black colour, well proportioned, squarle built, and no particular accidental Marks - Juda is about 48 years old black colour, about 5 feet high, square built, well proportioned and no particular accidental marks -
Whereupon it is ordered that a certificate thereof be awarded them according to Laws And the said Negroes Simon & Juda executed Bond as is reqd. by Law each in the Penalty of $300. Conditioned as the law directs with Leo Hayden their security.

A copy of George Ewing's Will can be found in Will Book A, p.67. The executors named in that will appeared in Court on this day to have their power of execution over the estate officially acknowledged. George Ewing decreed in his will that two of this slaves, Simon and Juda, were to be given their freedom at the time of his death. No manumission records have been found for them in the deed books, but in accordance with the Law of 1823, a physical description of each freed slave was officially recorded as is noted in the court record above. A complete copy of this court record can be found in the list of documents given for the case study: Simon.

Court Order Book E, p.45 [30]:

December Term 1845 It appearing to the Satisfaction of the court that James Frost departed this life in Wayne County Ky intestate more than three months ago and it also appearing to the Court that no person has applied for the Administration of the goods and chattles of said intestate estate. It is therefore ordered that Milton P. Buster Sheriff of Wayne County take Said estate into his possession and make Sale therof on a credit of twelve months (first giving public notice) taking from the purchaser or purchasers bond with a good security payable to himself as Sheriff of Wayne County; and that he make and return to this Court a true and perfect Inventory of the whole estate and an account of the Sales, together with the bonds &c hereby required to be taken

Executors of testate estates and administrators of intestate estates were required to have their positions confirmed by the courts, and these confirmations were recorded in the court order books. These records can be used to determine the date a will was officially probated, or they can be used to learn the identities of the administrator(s) appointed by the court for an intestate estate.

Court Order Book G, p.111 [31]:

Friday October 14th 1859
Petition for Division of Slaves:
  David Rankin Martha J. Rankin
  Samuel W. Gover Margaret E. Gover
  Matilda Gillespie William K.
    Gillespie

George T. Gillespie Samuel P. Gillespie
Mary Gillespie Thomas C. Gillespie
And James R. Wilhite

This day came the parties by their Attorney and produced and filed their Petition and on their motion it is Ordered that Thomas Copenhaver, A.H. Daugherty and William East be appointed Commissioners who being first duly Sworn for the purpose of making a division of the Slaves belonging to the estate of James G. Cowan dec'd refered to in the Petition between James R. Wilhite and the Other petitioners according to their value and the respective rights of said Petitioners and that one negro each out of the Gillespie Negroes be allotted to David Rankin and S.W. Gover at their appraised value which appraisment and valuation said Commissioners are required to make and report their actings and doings under this order in writing to this Court at its next term until which time this cause is continued.

Court Order Book G, p.122 [32]:

November Term 1859
Petition exparte for division of Slaves:
    David Rankin &c
        vs
    Gilespie Heirs

The Commissioners appointed at the last term of this Court to make partition and allotment of the Slaves named in the Petition this day made and filed their report and this action continued until the next term of this Court for the approval and confirmation of Said report & division.

This case is an example of an estate being held up in lengthy litigation. The case involved a dispute over the proper division of slaves belonging to the estate of William Gillespie, and in particular, a dispute over slaves formerly belonging to the Cowan family

which Gillespie claimed by right of marriage. The case can be followed through several terms of the court. The final decision regarding the division of the slaves of the disputed estate was recorded in detail on page 125 of Court Order Book G. A copy of this final court action can be found in the appendices of this book. Such disputed estate settlements when found in the Court Order Books, can be used in conjunction with probate and other records to help clarify relationships between the various members of a slaveowning family, relationships between the slaves and their new owners, and relationships between various slaves belonging to the estate.

Court Order Book F, p.247 [33]:

An inventory and appraisement of the estate of William Gillespie dec'd was this day produced to the Court filed and orderd to be recorded.
March Term 1855

This entry reveals that an inventory of the Gillespie estate was filed on this date. A subsequent search of the Inventory and Appraisement records located the said inventory with eight slaves listed therein.

Court Order Book K, p.331 [34]:

Ordered by the Court that James Vickory...Wash Daugherty (col.), George Copenhaver (col.), Prince Hinds (col.), James Ingram (col.), Josh Coil (col.), Abraham Garret (col.), Mike Coffey (col.), Alice Sheppard (col.) and...be and they are here by released from paying Poll Tax or County Levy on account of ill health &c 1889

It is wise to continue checking the court order books for a number of years after slavery was abolished. Once the former slaves received legal status as citizens, the search for any mention of them shifts from an investigation of the records pertaining to the former owners and focuses directly on the individuals themselves. For a great many years, black Americans continued to be distinguished in these records by the notation, colored (col.). From a strictly investigative standpoint, this designation makes locating individuals easier. The record above names a number of Wayne County citizens both black and white who were excused from paying taxes that year because of old age, poor health or some other legitimate reason.

## Evaluating the Tax Lists

From an early day most counties have had some form of annual taxation with accompanying annual taxation records. These tax records are a valuable source of complementary information often bypassed by the family historian. A great number of the early tax lists have survived, and they are being preserved on microfilm by various historical and genealogical associations. While the data provided by this particular record group serves mainly to complement information received from other sources, taxation lists can prove to be quite useful to the slave researcher.

The annual tax lists were kept on a county basis and remain a part of the county's archives. When working with these records it is important to check carefully the notations and headings of each individual list. Although the same basic information was recorded year after year, there was considerable variance from year to year in the actual recording of the data. As a rule only the total number of slaves was recorded along with an assessment of their total estimated market value. For a period of several years immediately preceding the Civil War, the taxation lists for Wayne County distinguished between slaves under 16 and those 16 & older.

Of principal value to our particular research problem, these annual tax lists serve as a complement to the decennial censuses. Whereas the first census available for Wayne County is the schedule of 1810, the county's taxation lists begin with 1801. Because slaves were recognized as taxable property, they were enumerated in these lists as part of each owner's taxable assets. Through these annual enumerations it is possible to identify any change in the number of slaves owned by a particular owner. When a change in the number of slaves is noted, the reseacher is alerted that he should check the county's deed books, court order books, and/or the probate records for the appropriate year(s) to locate a document to account for this change. Particular attention should be paid to the sudden appearance on these lists of any females. In almost all cases, such women were recent widows, and their appearance on the tax lists signals the researcher to search the appropriate probate records. Likewise, any sudden appearance of a "person of color" on these lists is a signal to check the deed books or court order books for some record of that person being freed within the preceding year.

Another purpose served by pre-1865 tax lists is to identify slaveowners who for one reason or another did not own any slaves at the time that the federal censuses were taken. Since the key to researching slave ancestors is to work through the records of their owners, it is imperative that no slaveowners be overlooked. When working with these records in the post-Civil War era, a very different perspective is needed.

It is important to know that after the war most Kentucky counties kept separate lists for whites and "coloreds." The same information was recorded in these separate lists, and the two records can usually be found side by side. The last three tax lists for Wayne County under slavery gave the following data on the county's black population: 1863, 4 free negroes & 932 slaves; 1864, 2 free negores & 932 slaves; 1865, no free negroes & 722 slaves [35]. The figures given in the 1860 census were: 28 'free colored' & 987 slaves [36]. No listings for blacks were found for 1866 or 1867. A "Colored Tax List" appeared for the first time in 1868, and accompanied the tax records given for the county's white citizenry.

Post-Civil War tax lists were often the first records to name former slaves, and they provide the black family historian with valuable information about his ancestors. As has been noted, a great number of blacks were missed on the 1870 and 1880 censuses. Tax lists are the best supplements to these. A comparison of the 1870 census with Wayne County's tax list for that year shows that there were a number of blacks appearing on the tax records who cannot be found on the census, and vice versa. Neither of these sources should ever be taken as conclusive, and comparisons should always be made between them. There were 112 black heads of households in the 1870 census, whereas there were 150 separate names on that year's "colored" tax list.

The early post-Civil War tax lists are also of special interest in that they record all taxable land owned by each person in the county. The researcher can use these records to approximate when a former slave first purchased his or her own land. Only one black, a female, Aggy Coffey, was listed with taxable real estate in 1868. Jack Coffey was added to the list of real estate holders in 1869, and Lank Kindrick was taxed on 20 acres in 1870 [37].

These early tax lists can also be used to help sketch a better profile of the various black families. Notations were made in these records for the number of childen in each taxpayer's household who were between the ages of 6 and 20. The number of females named on the tax lists will also want to be noted, as this is an indication that they headed up their own separate households at that time. Out of 170 blacks named on the 1868 tax lists, 14 were females. The list in 1869, consisted of 6 females out of 156 names, and in 1870 there were 4 females out of 150 black taxpayers [38]. As women usually dropped from the tax lists after marrying, the researcher will want to consider this possibility. It is interesting to note that the greatest number of black females appearing on the tax lists occurred on the list closest to the end of slavery.

## Additional Source Materials

Special attention has been given in this chapter to five major record groups found at the county level: vital records, probates, deeds, court orders, and tax lists. However, one's research is by no means completed with or limited to these sources. Any and every possible source of information should be investigated. Once a slave ancestor has been located and his or her owner has been identified, the researcher will want to learn all that can be discovered about that slave and slave's owner. The desire to truly identify and understand one's heritage does not allow one the luxury of investigating only certain aspects of that heritage. As Genovese points out, "Slavery...made white and black southerners one people while making them two. An understanding of the slaves requires some understanding of the masters and of others who helped shape a complex slave society. Masters and slaves shaped each other and cannot be discussed or analyzed in isolation." [39] As the various examples given in this study have illustrated, any investigation of the various records produced under slavery requires one to research the records of the slaves' owners. Similarly, a deeper and more comprehensive understanding of the slaveowning family can only help to broaden one's understanding and appreciation of one's slave ancestors and the world which they were forced to inhabit.

The researcher will want to become familiar with the locality where his ancestors lived, and a search should be made for any available histories written about the county or territory of interest. These histories should be studied not only for particular references to the families under investigation, those of the slaves and their owners, but also for a general understanding of the social, political, economic, religious and cultural enviroments in which they lived.

In addition to the county and local histories, one will also want to review any relevant family histories. While there are still relatively few black family histories available which extend back into the years of slavery, there is a very good possibility that a history has been written about the family of the slaveowner. Hopefully some mention will be made of the slaves bonded to this family, but even if that is not the case, the history can still provide the researcher with helpful information. To be able to trace the genealogy of slaves, one must be able to trace the genealogy of their owners. The Coffeys of Wayne County, (1974), is a good example of this [40]. While technically a history of one of Wayne County's pioneer white families, a number of references are made to the "Coffey" slaves. The book's appendices contain a variety of documents such as Coffey probate records which provide useful data on these slaves, and perhaps of even greater importance, this book untangles the numerous branches of this large family over a series of generations. With such an understanding of the familial makeup of this family, it is easier to speculate on how the Coffey slaves were distributed both inter- and intra-generationally within the Coffey family. This knowledge, of course, greatly facilitates the search for specific documents. Moreover, it was learned from this family history that there existed a special cemetery for the Coffey slaves located adjacent to the cemetery utilized by the Coffey family, and one reads about an epidemic of typhoid fever which struck and killed a number of Coffey slaves as well as members of the Coffey family over a two-year period beginning in the spring of 1853.

Church records are another potential source of information which should be surveyed. As a rule, the religious observances of most slaves, at least publicly, reflected the church affiliations of their owners. In 1860, the four largest religious bodies in Kentucky were: the Baptists - 250,000; Methodists - 200,000; Disciples - 100,000; and Presbyterians - 100,000 [41]. Strictly from a researcher's point of view, the predominance of these particular Protestant bodies, at least the first three, can prove to be disappointing, since these churches traditionally have kept few records of any real genealogical importance. Because there are, of course, exceptions to every rule, the researcher will want to survey any church histories or records

which may be available. Records of the Shearer Valley Church of Christ in Wayne County show that at least one former slave, Tamer J. Sallee, was a member of that congregation [42]. The Pleasant Hill Baptist Church founded in June 1841, had two blacks, Benjamin and Eady, as charter members [43]. The names of the nine white families originally associated with this congregation are also known, and one can safely assume that Benjamin and Eady were bonded to one of these families. A book on the history of the Baptist Churches of Wayne County reveals not only the name and location of the county's first "Negro" Baptist Church but also the name of the county's first black Baptist minister, Jonas Owsley [44]. Churches in the South, on a whole, reflected the opinions and feelings of the culture and society of which they were a part. Individual ministers and congregations did express their opposition to the institution of slavery, but their influence tended to be restricted to their own local communities. For the reader interested in learning more about the role played by the churches with regards to slavery, the following articles are recommended as a starting point for further study: Will Frank Steely, "The Established Churches and Slavery, 1850-1860," The Register of the Kentucky Historical Society, and Gaston Hugh Wamble, "Negroes and Missouri Protestant Churches Before and After the Civil War," Missouri Historical Review [45].

Although most slaves were buried in unmarked graves, there were some exceptions to this, and some of these marked graves can still be found. Unfortunately, only a relatively small number of county and family cemeteries in America have been surveyed and published to date, and even a smaller percentage of these cemetery indexes include listings for slaves. If a personal visit to the area of interest is at all possible, then a search can be made for any "missed" or "forgotten" markers. An extensive survey has recently been conducted of all known graves in Wayne County, and the findings of this survey have been published in Cemeteries of Wayne County, Kentucky, (1982). For the black family historian hoping to find a listing for his slave ancestors, this volume will prove disappointing. From a purely investigative perspective, any compilation of cemetery listings can prove useful. By knowing the birth and death dates of the various members of a slaveowning family, the researcher can better chart that family's genealogy and has a better chance of locating needed records such as probates.

The researcher will want to write to the public library and/or historical society in the county of interest and inquire about the availability of and the time span covered by the newspaper(s) in that locality. Many early newspapers have been microfilmed and are available for research. Of special interest to the black family historian would be advertisements of slave sales. Such advertisements usually included descriptions of the slaves for sale. Reports of runaways and notices of captured runaways were also published in the papers. In Kentucky, news about runaways statewide was published in the Lexington Gazette.

Anyone interested in researching more than one generation of Americans, as the family historian certainly is, must temper his research with the knowledge that America has never been a fixed entity. The America of any one generation has differed greatly from the America known by that generation's ancestors and descendants. From a physical perspective alone, the country has experienced almost continual changes in its boundaries, and the American people have rivaled the wind in their attempts to explore and conquer every corner of this vast land. Like the wind, this flood tide of humanity has often appeared to flow indiscriminately in all directions. Looking back with the advantage of time, we can see that definite patterns of movement and definite routes of migration have occurred. A knowledge of these patterns of American migration and settlement can aid the family historian in his efforts to track his family over a number of generations, and this is equally true for the black family historian as it is for whites. As Americans, and in particular, as

Southerners moved across the American frontier, black Americans willingly or not joined in this settlement of new lands. Many slaves simply accompanied their owners to these new territories. Many others became part of the growing domestic slave trade and were shipped off to new owners in these new lands. Either way, thousands of slaves were uprooted. To have a better chance of anticipating the movements of one's slave ancestors, some understanding of the principal patterns of migration is needed. A number of sources can provide the historian with this knowledge. Western Expansion, (5th ed. 1982), by Ray Allen Billington and Martin Ridge, can serve as one excellent reference source on this subject [46].

Another possible source of auxiliary information are the records of the Freedmen's Bureau. The Freedmen's Bureau was created by Congress during the final days of the Civil War and was set up to assist the former slaves in adjusting to their sudden status as free citizens. Bureau officials were sent south into the former slave states and charged with providing the former slaves with a number of diverse services. Some of these services included providing assistance in locating separated family members, assisting the freedmen in legal matters and in disputes over employment, investigating charges of brutality or harassment against the former slaves, assisting the ex-slaves in setting up schools, in obtaining food, clothing and housing, in purchasing land, and providing legal sanction to "slave marriages." A number of such unions were recognized by the Bureau, and certificates of marriage were given to these ex-slaves. Bureau officials likewise solemnized a number of new marriages between recently freed black Americans. The Bureau's influence in the South was short lived lasting in most cases only into 1868, and by 1872, the Bureau was abolished altogether. Bureau records have survived, but most are statistical with only fragmentary references to individuals. The only marriage records to survive which are of any real practical value to the family historian are those for Arkansas, Mississippi and the District of Columbus [47]. For a more detailed explanation of the Bureau, the reader is referred to, "Marriage Registers of Freedmen," Prologue: Journal of the National Archives [5] (Fall 1973), and "Records of Black Americans," Guide to Genealogical Research in the National Archives [48].

One final area of investigation for the black genealogists are military records. Black Americans have served their country during times of crises since a very early day. Slaves were often used in support services, but both slaves and free black Americans alike served their country bearing arms. During the Revolutionary War and later in the War of 1812, some slaves were offered freedom in return for military service. During the Civil War, slaves and former slaves could be found serving on both sides of the conflict. Many black Americans who served in a military capacity did so anonymously. Some did receive recognition, and there are records documenting their service. The historian who suspects that one of his ancestors may have served in the military will want to consult the current Guide to Genealogical Research in the National Archives to see what records are available. One such reference is the List of Black Servicemen Compiled from the War Department Collection of Revolutionary War Records [49]. For the descendant of black Kentuckians, "The Recruitment of Negro Soldiers in Kentucky, 1863-65," The Register of the Kentucky Historical Society [72] (Oct. 1974), should be of interest [50].

It is hoped that the data and discussions presented in this study will serve as a guide to those interested in tracing slave ancestry. As can be seen from the examples given, there is information available regarding these slaves. While some of the records and the methods for utilizing them are the same for all genealogical investigations, slave ancestry often requires special resources and special approaches. No one record will provide the researcher with all the information desired, but through an accumulation of many clues and bits of data a more complete portrait can be pieced together. To further illustrate some of the problems and procedures facing the black family historian, several case studies are presented in the next chapter on the developing of historical genealogies for several Wayne County slaves.

The unusual difficulties faced by the researchers of slave ancestry are not meant to be minimized, but it is the author's intention to show that while the problems facing the black family historian are indeed formidable, they are not always unsolvable. The challenges are great, but the rewards are even greater.

## CHAPTER III: CASE STUDIES

The following case studies have been chosen for the express purpose of illustrating the range of genealogical information that can be found for individual slaves and slave families and to illustrate how this assortment of information can be correlated to reveal a clearer profile of those slaves. While these case studies provide the historian with additional knowledge on the techniques of researching slave ancestry, it should be noted that one's actual research will not follow the exact same stages of investigation pursued in the case studies presented here. Every genealogical investigation is unique following the historical course of each particular family under study. Similarly, any actual genealogical investigation must follow a careful stage-by-stage development from the present to the past. As noted in the section on the preliminary survey in Chapter 1, the researcher must first ferret out all information located in one's own home and gather all possible information available on a family's most immediate members. No family's ancestry can be investigated properly until substantial information has been gathered on its more recent generations.

The case studies given here are simply examples of likely patterns of research at various possible stages of investigation. The author, being unrelated to and personally unfamiliar with any of the individuals considered in these studies, has not had the advantage of possessing any of the supplementary information normally available to the family historian. It has not been possible to follow the natural course of investigation of specific families generation by generation from the present

back to their slave ancestors. Consequently the examples given in these case studies suffer from being chronologically isolated.

None of these case studies represents a "completed" family history. It is hoped that as the reader scans through these studies, he or she will consider a number of additional sources which should be consulted and will envision a number of additional potential research paths which should be pursued.

### Case Study One: Milly Copenhaver

Milly Copenhaver is an example of the records showing a slave being owned over a relatively short period of time by several different members of a single family. The year of Milly's birth can only be approximated. One record, a deed of gift filed in 1843, would suggest that Milly had been born as late as 1827, but a review of all accumulated data would suggest 1820-1823 being the more likely range.

The first record found referring to the legal transfer of the slave Milly from one owner to another was a deed of gift, Deed Book I, p. 64 (a copy of this deed can be found in Appendix B: Deeds of Gift). In September of 1843, Christopher Simpson gave his two granddaughters Catherine and Elizabeth Copenhaver a certain negro girl named Milly about 16 years old and her baby named James about 10 months old. The slaves were given to Catherine and Elizabeth as an outright gift as an expression of their grandfather's love, and the girls were to share equally in the ownership of these slaves. Catherine and Elizabeth were the daughters of Thomas Copenhaver, a prominent Methodist minister and farmer in Wayne County. A check of the Wayne County marriage records reveals that Thomas Copenhaver was married in January 1828, to Christopher Simpson's daughter Nancy. Census records show that their daughter Catherine was born in 1828/1829, and Elizabeth was born in 1830/1831. Thomas Copenhaver remarried in August 1835, to Elizabeth Barnes, so his first wife, Nancy Simpson, died sometime between 1831-1835. Elizabeth Copenhaver was married in January 1845 to Aaron T. Woolsey, and her older sister Catherine was married in June 1851 to Barton W. S. Mercer [51].

Deed Book L, p. 268 (a copy of this deed can be found in Appendix B: Bills of Sale) shows that in 1851, Elizabeth and her husband Aaron Woolsey sold their half ownership of the slave Milly to Elizabeth's father Thomas Copenhaver. The researcher learns from the information given in this bill of sale that in addition to her son James mentioned in the deed of gift recorded in 1843, the slave Milly had had two additional children in the intervening years, a son Tom and a daughter Amy Elizabeth. Milly's age in this later deed was given as 30, and the ages of her three children were given as James 8, Tom 6, and Amy Elizabeth 4. All four slaves were described as being of a black color. Aaron and Elizabeth Woolsey sold their half ownership of Milly and her three children for $500.00.

Also of importance to the researcher, this deed reveals that the slaves in question while legally belonging to Elizabeth and Catherine had nevertheless remained in the actual possession of Thomas Copenhaver. This tells the researcher that he should expect to find Milly and her children listed under the owner Thomas Copenhaver in the 1850 slave schedule. This appears to be the case. (See Chart 4.)

A search was made of the 1850 and 1860 slave schedules for owners who might have had some link to the slave Milly. Few definite conclusions can be reached by using these statistical schedules alone, but they can provide the researcher with hopeful hypotheses.

The listings for several pertinent slaveowners are given below. (See Chart 5.)

CHART 4

1850 Slave Schedule

owner:        slaves: age/sex/color

Thomas Copenhaver 30 F B (Milly)
                  17 M B
                  14 M B
                   7 M B (James)
                   6 M B (Tom)
                   4 F B (Amy Elizabeth)

No record has yet been found revealing the names of Milly's parents. Since Milly was still relatively young when she was first given away by Christopher Simpson in 1843, it is reasonable to speculate that Milly was a daughter of one of Simpson's slaves. In 1850, Christopher Simpson was recorded as owning a female slave 45 years old. Christopher Simpson died before the next census, and it appears that the 60-year-old female slave owned by Thomas Simpson in 1860 was the same slave owned earlier by Christopher. Whether this slave had been born in 1800 or in 1805, she was of a feasible age to have been Milly's mother. Because it appears that this female slave remained a permanent member of the Simpson "household," no deed has been found giving her name, and no record as yet has been located revealing her identity. Likewise, no practical speculations can presently be made on the identity of Milly's father.

Milly was approximately 43 years old when slavery in America came to an end. The following entry was found for Milly in the 1870 census. (See Chart 6.)

Looking at this 1870 census entry, it is first noted that Milly chose, or was given, the surname Copenhaver even though at various times in her life she had at least two owners with different names, Simpson and Woolsey. Since the relationships between the various members of a household were not specified in the 1870 census, one can only speculate on what those relationships might

CHART 5

## 1850 Slave Schedule

| owner: | slaves: | age/sex/color | | | owner: | slaves: | age/sex/color | | |
|---|---|---|---|---|---|---|---|---|---|
| Aaron T. Woolsey | | 7 | M | B | Lavina Copenhaver* | | 46 | F | B |
| | | | | | | | 31 | F | B |
| Christopher Simpson | | 45 | F | B | | | 23 | M | Mu |
| | | 24 | M | Mu | | | 30 | M | B |
| | | 14 | F | B | | | 15 | F | B |
| | | 5 | F | B | | | 13 | F | B |
| | | | | | | | 10 | F | B |
| David Simpson | | 18 | F | B | | | 10 | F | B |
| | | 7 | F | B | | | 8 | M | B |
| | | | | | | | 6 | M | B |
| | | | | | | | 4 | M | B |
| | | | | | | | 3 | M | B |

*Lavina was Thomas' mother

## 1860 Slave Schedule

| owner: | slaves: | age/sex/color | | | owner: | slaves: | age/sex/color | | |
|---|---|---|---|---|---|---|---|---|---|
| Thomas Copenhaver | | 37 | F | B (Milly) | Thomas Simpson | | 60 | F | B |
| | | 26 | M | B | | | | | |
| | | 22 | M | B | David Simpson | | 30 | M | Mu |
| | | 20 | F | B | | | 28 | F | B |
| | | 17 | M | B (James) | | | 14 | M | B |
| | | 16 | F | B | | | 11 | F | B |
| | | 14 | M | B (Tom ?) | | | 10 | M | B |
| | | 13 | F | B (Amy Elizabeth) | | | 6 | M | Mu |
| | | 9 | M | B | | | | | |
| | | 8 | F | B | B.W.S. Mercer | | 16 | M | B |
| | | 6 | F | B | | | 13 | F | B |

Lavina Copenhaver had 27 slaves in the 1860 Schedule with ages from 58 to 2.

## CHART 6

### 1870 Census

Mill Spring, p.16

|  |  | color | age | birthplace | occupation |
|---|---|---|---|---|---|
| #114- | Copenhaver, Milly | B | 47 | KY | keeps house |
| " | , Elizabeth | B | 22 | " |  |
| " | , Stephen | B | 9 | " |  |
| " | , James | B | 27 | " | farm laborer |
| " | , Catherine | B | 22 | " |  |

## CHART 7

### 1880 Census

E.D. 105, p.4

|  |  | color | age | marital status | relation-ship | birthplace "/father/mother | | |
|---|---|---|---|---|---|---|---|---|
| #28-28 | Copenhaver, Bob | B | 33 | widow | head | KY | KY | KY |
| " | , Milly | B | 60 | widow | -- | " | " | " |
| " | , William | B | 8 | single | son | " | " | " |
| " | , Mattie | B | 6 | " | dau. | " | " | " |

## CHART 8

### 1870 Census

Mill Spring, p.4

|  |  | color | age | birthplace | occupation |
|---|---|---|---|---|---|
| #25 | Copenhaver, Robert G. | B | 23 | KY | farmer |
| " | , Nancy E. | B | 16 | " |  |
| " | , William | B | 14 | " | farm laborer |

# GENEALOGY OF MILLY COPENHAVER (SLAVE)

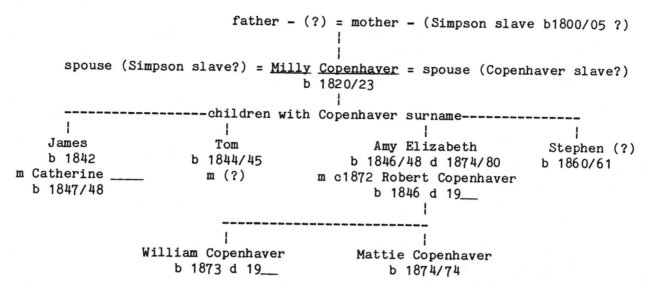

```
                    father - (?) = mother - (Simpson slave b1800/05 ?)
                                 |
                                 |
      spouse (Simpson slave?) = Milly Copenhaver = spouse (Copenhaver slave?)
                                    b 1820/23
                                 |
         ------------------children with Copenhaver surname---------------
         |                    |                     |                    |
       James                 Tom              Amy Elizabeth          Stephen (?)
       b 1842             b 1844/45         b 1846/48 d 1874/80       b 1860/61
     m Catherine ____       m (?)       m c1872 Robert Copenhaver
       b 1847/48                             b 1846 d 19__
                                                  |
                          ---------------------------
                          |                         |
                  William Copenhaver          Mattie Copenhaver
                     b 1873 d 19__               b 1874/74
```

NOTE: Milly's son-in-law, Robert Copenhaver, and her grandson, William Copenhaver, were found in the 1900 Census in Wayne County. Robert Copenhaven married 2nd in 1883 Martha ___ (b 1863 d 19--) and had four additional children.


# GENEALOGY OF THE OWNERS OF THE SLAVE, MILLY COPENHAVER

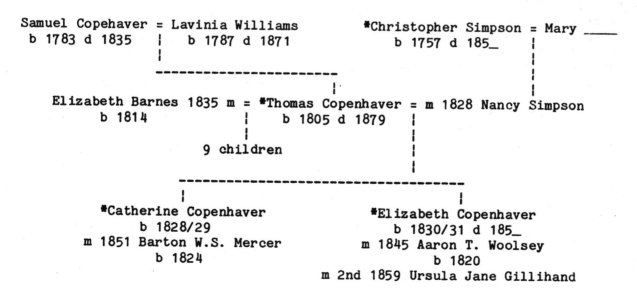

```
  Samuel Copehaver = Lavinia Williams        *Christopher Simpson = Mary ____
    b 1783 d 1835  |   b 1787 d 1871            b 1757 d 185_      |
                   |                                              |
                   |                                              |
         -----------------------                                 |
         |                     |                                 |
 Elizabeth Barnes 1835 m = *Thomas Copenhaver = m 1828 Nancy Simpson
    b 1814              |     b 1805 d 1879    |
                        |                      |
                   9 children                 |
                        |                      |
         ------------------------------------------------
         |                                    |
  *Catherine Copenhaver              *Elizabeth Copenhaver
     b 1828/29                          b 1830/31 d 185_
   m 1851 Barton W.S. Mercer          m 1845 Aaron T. Woolsey
     b 1824                             b 1820
                                      m 2nd 1859 Ursula Jane Gillihand
```

NOTE: the slave Milly Copenhaven was owned at various times by at least three generations of the Simpson/Copenhaven family. Her owners mentioned in the case study are marked by an (*) in the chart.

41

have been. Elizabeth, age 22, was undoubtedly Milly's daughter who was listed in the 1851 bill of sale as the 4-year-old slave girl named Amy Elizabeth. James was surely Milly's oldest son, and Catherine, age 22, was very likely James' wife. The identity of the 9-year-old boy Stephen is unknown. It seems safe to rule out his being the son of either Elizabeth or Catherine, and one may speculate on the possibility of his being a much younger son of Milly. Her second son Tom who should have been about 25 years old was not listed with the family and was not found in the 1870 census. Two separate Tom Copenhavers were found ten years later in the 1880 census, one 36 years old and the other 37. Milly Copenhaver was not found in the first Wayne County "colored" tax list in 1868, but her son James Copenhaver was listed along with 12 other black Copenhaver tax entries, including two Tom Copenhavers, one labeled in the list as Tom "Long" and the other Tom "Short."

The census provides the researcher with no helpful clues as to the identity of the father(s) of Milly's children. Milly was obviously not living with the children's father when the census was taken. Since Milly's oldest child James was born while they were still part of the Simpson slaves, it is possible, although by no means proven, that Milly's later children and her first child James were sired by different fathers.

The census in 1880 provides the researcher with an assortment of answers and also additional questions. (See Chart 7.)

In 1880, Milly was no longer listed as the head of a household but was found living in the home of Bob Copenhaver. Both Bob and Milly were listed as being widowed, but the relationship between them was not stated. William and Mattie were listed as Bob's children. The most obvious conclusion to be drawn from this entry is that Bob had been married to Milly's daughter Amy Elizabeth, and Bob was Milly's son-in-law. Neither James, who would have been about 37, nor Stephen, who should have been about 19, were located in the 1880 census.

Milly's son-in-law, Bob Copenhaver, was found in the 1870 census, but no clues as to his parents' identities can be drawn from that single census entry. It is plausible to assume that Bob had been a slave to either Thomas Copenhaver or his mother Lavina, and one may venture to assume that Bob and his future wife Elizabeth first met and became enamored with one another while bonded by slavery to the Copenhaver family. (See Chart 8.)

The white Copenhaver family was one of the more substantial slaveowning families of Wayne County, and a great number of former Wayne County slaves chose to adopt the surname Copenhaver after their emancipation. This profuseness of the name makes research of the Copenhaver slaves somewhat more difficult, but hopefully even this rather cursory investigation of just one Copenhaver slave has shown that research is possible. As was noted in the main body of the book, a wide variety of sources can and should be investigated, and the search to uncover the history of Milly Copenhaver's family is by no means limited to the sources and documents mentioned here. The family historian's research is an unending process.

## Case Study Two: Cowan-Gillespie Slaves

Mention has been made in the discussion on the use of court order books to the litigation concerning the proper distribution of the slaves belonging to the heirs of the Cowan-Gillespie estate. Additional information concerning this case is also found in Appendices A & C. A number of slaves and slaveowners are mentioned in these court documents and related probate records, and an effort shall be made in the following case study to correlate the information contained in these documents with data from other record sources.

As noted in the Cemeteries of Wayne County, Kentucky, William Gillespie died on February 21, 1855. His will written two months earlier was probated a few days after his death (an abstracted copy of the will can be found in Appendix A). Gillespie's will names eight slaves and specifies their familial relationships. Although slave marriages had no legal status in the antebellum South, Gillespie's will does specify that the slave Rebecca was the slave Perry's "wife." It is interesting to note, however, that the two slave boys Isaac and William are listed as being Rebecca's children rather than being the children of both Perry and Rebecca. Two additional female slaves are named, each having one child: Rose with her son Lewis and Lucinda with her son Green. Following the norm of documents pertaining to the slavery era no indication is given as to the identity of the children's father(s).

The appraised market value of these slaves listed in the estate's official appraisement and inventory (Appendix A) shows that the three female slaves were all appraised at the same price, $700. This would normally indicate that they were roughly within the same age category, and the fact that they were all the mothers of either one or two young children seems to confirm this. The highest valuation of $900 belonged to the single adult male Perry, and the valuations for the slave children ranged from $800 for William, $500 each for Isaac and Green, and $200 for Lewis. The most logical assumption that the researcher can make concerning these prices for the children is that they reflected their ages. A check of Wayne County's surviving vital records for the early 1850's shows that a Gillespie slave named Lewis was born on October 15, 1852. If this was the same Lewis appraised at $200, then he would have been two years old at the time the inventory was taken. A search of the censuses for 1870 and 1880 located black men named, William, Isaac and Green Gillespie, and assuming that these men were the same slave boys referred to above, their ages at the time of the inventory of 1855 would have been approximately eight years old for William, and six years old for both Isaac and Green. These ages correspond with the slaves' varying appraised market valuations.

Birth and death records for Wayne County survive for the years 1852-1858,

and these were checked for any mention of Gillespie slaves. The death of the slave boy Lewis was recorded in September 1855. He was listed as being three years old, black of color, a native of Wayne County, and a slave of William Gillespie. His mother's name was not given, and the cause of death was listed as unknown. A female slave named Alvis was born in October 1856 to the slave woman Rosey, and both were listed as property of William Gillespie's widow Nancy.

Gillespie bequeathed his slaves to his wife Nancy, and further specified that upon her death they be equally divided amongst their children. William Gillespie referred in his will to additional slaves belonging to his mother-in-law, Nancy Cowan. He did not specify the number of Cowan slaves involved nor did he identify them in any way. Gillespie assumed that these Cowan slaves would be inherited by his family and made provisions in his will for them. Both of his executors, who were also his sons-in-law David Rankin and Samuel Gover, were to receive one of these slaves, and they were commissioned by him to supervise the remaining slaves for the benefit and general welfare of the estate. The balance of Gillespie's children were to receive an equal or equivalent share of the estate's assets as they became of age. Gillespie stipulated that the slaves for their "comfort ad well being" were to remain in the family as long as they were well behaved. Any refractory slaves were to be hired out by the executors until they made amends.

To attempt to track any of these slaves belonging to the Gillespie-Cowan estate, the researcher must first be able to chart the family of the slaves' owners. William and Nancy Gillespie were married in Wayne County on May 21, 1828. Nancy was the daughter of James G. and Nancy Cowan who had come to Kentucky from Virginia. A younger daughter of the Cowans named Martha was married in 1840, to James R. Wilhite. The Cowans probably had other children besides Nancy and Martha, but it was these two Cowan daughters and their families who figured in the litigation over the distribution of the Cowan slaves. William and Nancy Gillespie were the parents of ten children as shown on the Genealogical Chart of the Cowan-Gillespie Family [52].

James G. Cowan died in 1852. His son-in-law, William Gillespie died in 1855. Both were listed as slaveowners in the 1850 slave schedule, as was James R. Wilhite. (See Chart 9.)

CHART 9

1850 Slave Schedule

| owner: | slaves: | age/sex/color | |
|--------|---------|------|----|
| James G. Cowan | 36 | M | Mu |
| | 27 | M | Mu |
| | 24 | M | B |
| | 18 | M | B |
| | 60 | F | B |
| | 55 | F | B |
| | 24 | F | B |
| | 22 | F | B |
| | 8 | F | B |
| | 5 | M | B |
| | 1 | M | B |
| William Gillespie | 30 | M | B |
| | 23 | F | B |
| | 20 | F | B |
| | 2 | F | B |
| James R. Wilhite | 15 | F | B |

Cowan's widow, Nancy, died sometime between 1856-1859. Her death necessitated court action to settle the distribution of her estate. A petition for division of the estate's slaves was filed on October 14, 1859. The court appointed Thomas Copenhaver, A. H. Daugherty and William East as Commissioners to evaluate the present status of the estate of the late James G. Cowan (Court Order Book G, p.111). It is interesting to note that all three court appointed commissioners were themselves slaveowners. Experience in working with the estate papers of slaveowners has shown that administrators, commissioners or any other officials appointed by the courts to deal in any way with the prop-

erty or estate of one slaveowner were almost always slaveowners themselves. The researcher will want to remember this practice as one more aid to assist in the identifying of a county's slaveowners.

A final court settlement was recorded December 1859, in Wayne County's Court Order Book G, p.125 (a copy of this court record is given in Appendix C). James R. Wilhite and the Gillespie executors figure prominently in this court action, and the proposed distribution of the Cowan slaves is outlined. No mention is made of William Gillespie's widow, Nancy, since William had devised in his will that the Cowan slaves were to pass on to their children. Thirteen Cowan slaves were mentioned in this settlement with seven going to James R. Wilhite, one each to Samuel Gover and David Rankin, and four to Rankin and Gover as executors of the Gillespie estate.

December 1859, Court ordered settlement of Cowan estate:

slaves to James R. Wilhite –
   Lucinda & young child
   Garrett
   Henry
   Bezeal
   Charles
   Ceasar
to the heirs of Wm. Gillespie –
   Eliza
   Bob
   Morris
   Sarah
to David Rankin –
   Louis, valued at $1,200
to Samuel W. Gover –
   John

This new alignment in the slaves is somewhat illustrated in the 1860 slave schedule. It is important to remember that these census schedules only reflect the slaves owned at one particular isolated time. (See Chart 10.)

An attempt was made to locate these former slaves in early post-emancipation documents. It was assumed that they adopted one of the following surnames: Cowan, Gillespie, Rankin, Gover or

Wilhite. The 1868-1870 Wayne County tax lists were searched, and the following "colored" taxpayers were found for those years. (See Chart 11.)

## CHART 10

### 1860 Slave Schedule

| owner: | slaves: | age/sex/color | |
|---|---|---|---|
| Samuel Gover | 15 | M | B |
| Samuel Gover | 30 | F | B |
| & 7 others | 8 | F | B |
| (heirs of the | 6 | M | B |
| Gillespie estate) | 3 | M | B |
| James R. Wilhite | 46 | M | Mu |
| | 33 | M | B |
| | 26 | F | B |
| | 26 | F | Mu |
| | 24 | F | B |
| | 18 | F | Mu |
| | 10 | M | B |
| | 8 | M | B |
| | 9 | F | Mu |
| | 6 | M | B |
| | 7 | F | Mu |
| | 4 | M | Mu |
| | 4 | M | B |
| | 4 | F | Mu |
| | 2 | M | Mu |
| | 8/12 | M | B |
| | 4/12 | M | Mu |
| | 1/12 | M | Mu |
| | 65 | F | B |
| | 60 | F | B |

3 slave houses

| David Rankin | 25 | M | B |
|---|---|---|---|
| Nancy Gillespie | 35 | M | Mu |
| | 29 | F | B |
| | 30 | F | B |
| | 15 | M | Mu |
| | 11 | M | B |
| | 13 | M | Mu |
| | 4 | F | Mu |
| | 2 | M | B |
| | 11 | F | B |

A search of the 1870 and 1880 censuses was only partially rewarding. Of the eight slaves mentioned in William Gillespie's will in 1854, only William and Isaac were located in 1870, and only William and Green were found in 1880. In all of these entries these former slaves used the surname Gillespie or some spelling variant of it. No slaves were found using the surname Gover. Although Perry Gillespie was found in the tax lists, he did not appear on the 1870 census. (See Chart 12.)

## CHART 11

### WAYNE COUNTY TAX LISTS

#### 1868

Gillespie, Perry
  "    , Isaac
  "    , Rose
  "    , William
Wilhite, Cesar
  "    , Charles
Rankin, Joseph
  "    , Lewis

#### 1869

Gillespie, Perry
  "    , William
  "    , Green*
Cowan, Cesar
Rankin, Edward
  "    , Lewis
  "    , Joseph

#### 1870

Gillespie, Perry
  "    , William
  "    , Isaac
  "    , Rosey
  "    , Green*
Rankin, Lewis
  "    , Joseph
  "    , Nelson
Whilhite, Charles
  "    , Braziel

* Green Gillespie was listed in the lower district; all others were in the upper district.

# CHART 12

## 1870 Census

Mill Spring, p.11                           Mill Spring, p.19

78- Gillespie, Isaac 22 B Farmer KY    130- Gillespie, William 23 B Farmer KY
    "       , Mary  18 B         "              "      , Lucy     23 B        "
                                                "      , Martha    2 B

-----------------------------

## 1880 Census

MillSprings, p.26

| 222-232 | Gilaspie, William | 34 | B | farmer | KY | KY | KY |
|---------|-------------------|----|----|--------|----|----|----|
| " | , Lucey J. | 37 | B | wife | VA | VA | VA |
| " | , Mary C. | 14 | B | dau. | KY | KY | " |
| " | , Rebeckey J. | 9 | B | " | " | " | " |
| " | , Marthy | 6 | B | " | " | " | " |
| " | , Lueverney | 5 | B | " | " | " | " |
| " | , Eddy J. | 3 | B | " | " | " | " |
| " | , William | 1 | B | son | " | " | " |

MillSprings, p.27

| 238-248 | Gilaspie, Green | 32 | B | farmer | KY | KY | KY |
|---------|-----------------|----|----|--------|----|----|----|
| " | , Mariah J. | 27 | B | wife | TN | TN | TN |
| " | , Allmarin | 11 | B | son | TN | SC | TN |
| " | , Evey | 9 | B | dau. | " | " | " |
| " | , Tien | 7 | B | " | KY | KY | " |

Three of the former Cowan slaves involved in the court action of 1859 were found living together in 1870. It is noted that all three of these former Cowan slaves went by the name Rankin in this 1870 entry. The slaves Lewis and Morris had been allotted to David Rankin in 1859, but Bazeal had been among those slaves allotted to James R. Wilhite. (See Chart 13.)

CHART 13

1870 Census

Mill Spring p. 19

```
135- Rankin,Lewis    30 B farmer      KY
      "   ,Barzeal   19 B farm laborer KY
      "   ,Morris    12 B  "     "     KY
```

The slave Ceasar was also one of the Cowan slaves allotted in 1859 to James Wilhite. The first "colored" tax list of 1868 shows this ex-slave listed as Cesar Wilhite. The following year and there after, he was listed as Cesar Cowan. It is interesting to note that Ceasar chose to return to this earlier surname, and a possible explanation for this action will be proffered later in this study. Ceasar was listed in both the 1870 and 1880 censuses as Cowan, and those of his descendants located in 1900 continued to adhere to this name. (See Chart 14.)

A search of the 1852-1858 vital records revealed two entries pertaining to the family of Ceasar. In the first entry dated May 1854, a slave boy named Robinson was born to a slave woman named Caroline who was owned by Nancy Cowan. On June 1, 1858, a boy named Asberry was born to the slave Caroline who was at that time listed as being owned by James R. Wilhite. No pertinent slave deaths were found for this same period. It would appear that Ceasar's wife Caroline and at least some of her children passed directly from the Cowans to the Wilhites without being part of the contested estate settlement.

Looking back at the 1850 slave schedule, it would appear that Ceasar was the 35-year-old male mulatto slave owned by James G. Cowan. In the 1860 schedule Ceasar would have been the 46-year-old male mulatto owned by James R. Wilhite. Because of the discrepancies in Caroline's age, it is harder to pinpoint exactly which of the female slaves she was. Logical choices would be the Wilhite's 33-year-old female slave in 1860, and either Cowan's 24- or 22-year-old female slave in 1850. Of interest to anyone investigating Ceasar Cowan and his family would be the two middle-aged female slaves listed first under James Cowan in 1850, and later under James Wilhite in the 1860 schedule. Either one of these women could feasibly have been Ceasar's mother. A black female named Venus Cowan was found in the 1870 census aged 100. Remembering that very few slaves had any real knowledge of their exact ages, and given the wide discrepancies found in the census data, Venus could conceivably have been the female Cowan slave listed as being 60 years old in 1850. Venus Cowan was recorded in the census as having been born in Virginia which corresponds to the given birthplace of Ceasar's mother. Venus's relationship to the other members of the household in which she was living in 1870, has not as yet been determined. Both a Gillespie (Gelaspie) and a Wilhite were members of this same household in 1880. Venus and Ceasar were listed as close neighbors in the 1870 census. If Venus Cowan was indeed Ceasar's mother, then that could possibly explain his decision to abandon the name Wilhite in favor of the name used by his mother. No clues as to the identity of Ceasar's father have been uncovered other than the fact that Ceasar was consistently classified as being a mulatto, and the 1880 census listed both of Ceasar's parents as having been born in Virginia. Keeping these two points in mind, the researcher should at least consider the possibility of the slaveowner, James Cowan, being Ceasar's father. (See Chart 15.)

Ceasar's widow, Caroline, was found living alone in the 1900 census. She answered that she was the mother of ten children, five of whom were still living. The month and year of her birth

## CHART 14

### 1870 Census

Mill Spring, p.17

| 123- | Cowan, Ceasar | 56 | Mu | farmer | VA |
|------|---------------|----|----|--------|-----|
| | " , Caroline | 39 | Mu | | KY |
| | " , Amanda | 15 | Mu | | " |
| | " , Beckie | 13 | Mu | | " |
| | " , Asberry | 12 | Mu | farm laborer | " |
| | " , Isaac | 9 | B | | " |
| | " , Robert G. | 1 | Mu | | " |

### 1880 Census

Millspring, p.8

| 73-74 | Cow, Sezar | 65 | B | farmer | VA | VA | VA | |
|-------|------------|----|----|--------|-----|-----|-----|--|
| | " , Caroline | 43 | B | wife | KY | KY | KY | |
| | " , Asbery* | 21 | B | son | " | " | " | works on farm |
| | " , Rebecky | 23 | B | dau. | " | " | " | |
| | " , Isac P. | 19 | B | son | " | " | " | works on farm |
| | " , Magalien | 8 | B | dau. | " | " | " | |

* Asbery Cowan was found listed twice in the 1880 Census. He was listed as part of the household of John Wilhite (Millspring p. 23, 198-206).

John Wilhite was a 30 year old white farmer, and Asbery Cowan was listed as a boarder who worked on the Wilhite farm. John Wilhite was a son of Ceasar Cowan's former owner, James R. Wilhite.

## CHART 15

### 1870 Census

Millspring p. 18

### 1880 Census

Millspring p. 5

| 127- | Jones, Charles | 32 | B | KY | 46-46 | Jones, Charles | 41 | B | farmer | KY | KY | KY |
|------|----------------|----|----|----|-------|----------------|----|----|--------|-----|-----|-----|
| | " , Sarelda J. | 26 | Mu | " | | " , Sureldy J. | 36 | Mu | wife | " | " | " |
| | " , William P. | 10 | Mu | " | | " , Wm. P. | 19 | Mu | son | " | " | " |
| | Cowan, Venus | 100 | B | VA | | Hutchison, Coata (f) | 19 | B | cozen | " | " | " |
| | Shelton, Marsh | 30 | B | KY | | Gelaspie, Joney (m) | 10 | B | nephew | " | " | " |
| | " , Sarah | 18 | B | " | | Willhite, Charles H. | 1 | Mu | " | " | " | " |

# GENEALOGY OF THE COWAN-GILLESPIE FAMILY (SLAVE OWNERS)

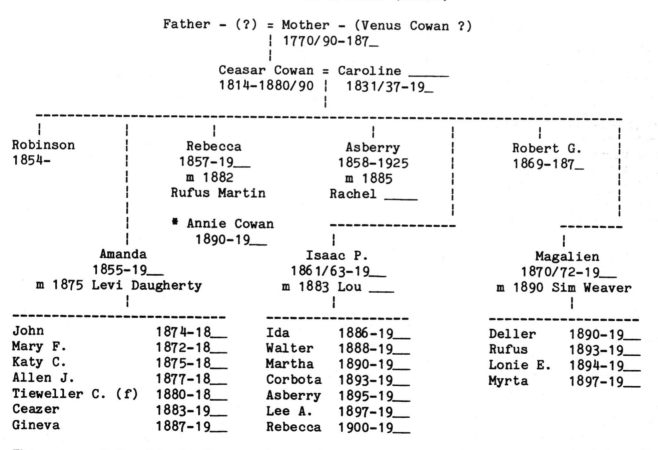

```
                    James G. Cowan = Nancy _____
                     1783-1852     |  c1780-1856/59
                                   |
                 ----------------------------------------
                        |                         |
   William  Gillespie = Nancy Cowan    James R. Wilhite = Martha Cowan
    1808-1855 m 1828  | 1810-1885       1814-1878 m 1840   1819-1890
                      |
           Martha Jane  1831-1896, m. 1851, David Rankin 1828-1900
           Margaret E.  1833-1910, m. 1853, Samuel W. Gover 1830-1913
           Robert       1835-185_
           John G.      1838-1857
           Matilda      1842-
           William      1844-
           George T.    1846-1868
           Samuel B.    1848-
           Thomas C.    1850-1870
           Mary         1853-1881
```

## GENEALOGY OF CESAR COWAN (SLAVE)

```
          Father - (?) = Mother - (Venus Cowan ?)
                       | 1770/90-187_
                       |
                Ceasar Cowan = Caroline _____
                 1814-1880/90 | 1831/37-19_
                              |
   -------------------------------------------------------------------
     |          |          |                |            |          |
  Robinson      |       Rebecca           Asberry        |     Robert G.  |
   1854-        |      1857-19__          1858-1925       |    1869-187_   |
                |       m 1882            m 1885          |                |
                |     Rufus Martin        Rachel ____     |                |
                |                                         |                |
                |   * Annie Cowan    ----------------     --------         |
                |     1890-19__            |                    |
           Amanda                      Isaac P.             Magalien
          1855-19__                  1861/63-19__          1870/72-19__
      m 1875 Levi Daugherty          m 1883 Lou ___       m 1890 Sim Weaver
                |                         |                    |
   ------------------------    -------------------    -------------------
   John            1874-18__   Ida       1886-19__    Deller   1890-19__
   Mary F.         1872-18__   Walter    1888-19__    Rufus    1893-19__
   Katy C.         1875-18__   Martha    1890-19__    Lonie E. 1894-19__
   Allen J.        1877-18__   Corbota   1893-19__    Myrta    1897-19__
   Tieweller C. (f)1880-18__   Asberry   1895-19__
   Ceazer          1883-19__   Lee A.    1897-19__
   Gineva          1887-19__   Rebecca   1900-19__
```

The names of Caroline's three other children are not known, but it is assumed they died young.

* Annie Cowan, born in 1890, was living in 1900 with her Aunt Rebecca.

were left blank. She and her parents were listed as natives of Kentucky. Caroline was listed next to Sim and Maggie Weaver. Maggie was given as being born in October 1870. She answered that her father had been born in Virginia and her mother in Kentucky. She was the mother of four children, all still living. Maggie and Sim had been married ten years. It seems safe to speculate that Maggie Weaver was Ceasar and Caroline's daughter listed as Magalien in the 1880 census. Their daughter Amanda Cowan was married in 1875 to Levi Daugherty. Both appear in the 1900 census with the two surviving of their seven children. Another daughter Rebecca was found in 1900 living with her husband of 18 years, Rufus Martin. They had no children of their own but had a ten-year-old niece, Annie Cowan, living with them. Ceasar's sons, Asberry and Isaac Cowan, were also located in the 1900 census. Asberry and his wife Rachel had no children, while Isaac and his wife Lou had seven, all still alive. All of the individuals listed above were found in the 1900 census in E.D. 131 and were near neighbors in the Mill Spring section of Wayne County [53]. As noted in Cemeteries of Wayne County, Kentucky, tombstones have been found for Asberry Cowan and his wife Rachel, and are located at the Mt. Zion A.M.E. Church Cemetery.

Using the information discussed in this case study an outline of Ceasar Cowan's family can be sketched. A more complete genealogy of the slave Ceasar and his family would require a much more extensive survey of all available records pertaining to any of these slaves' possible owners. The researcher would of course want to check the deed books for any acquisition or disposal of any slave(s) by all of these potential owners, and one would need to conduct a careful survey of the county's annual tax lists. Since Ceasar was listed as having been born in Virginia, anyone interested in his ancestry would want to track the white Cowan family back to their own roots in that state. The possibilities for further research into the family histories of any of these Cowan-Gillespie slaves are as limitless

as the researcher's imagination, experience and determination.

## Case Study Three:
## Simon, commonly called Si

Although an effort has been made in the selection of these case studies to choose suitable subjects on a strictly academic basis, the author acknowledges that personal considerations have somewhat influenced the selection of this last subject. While working through Wayne County's various records the name of one black man was encountered on a number of occasions. As the references to this individual mounted, he succeeded in capturing the author's interest and imagination. An attempt was made to gather more information on this man and his family, and a respectable variety of records were located to make them worthy subjects of a case study. The man in question was referred to by a number of different names over the years, but one particular appellation was most frequently encountered, and it seems apparent after reading through a number of documents that most residents of Wayne County knew him as such. The subject of this case study then shall be referred to as he was most often referred to by his own neighbors. Case Study Three is dedicated to the slave "Simon, commonly called Si."

One of the factors causing Si to be of special interest is the fact that he is one of those rare slaves of whom we have a physical description. In accordance with Kentucky's Law of 1823 regarding the manumission of slaves within that state, physical descriptions of both Si and his wife Juda were officially recorded by the Wayne County court at the time of their emancipation. As all family historians well know, one of the most treasured links one can establish with someone from the past is to be able in some way to visualize an ancestor's physical appearance. This most personal of all documentation is also the most rare.

Wayne County, Kentucky Court Order Book D, p.35 (Film 591,544):

January Court 1839

At a County Court began and held for Wayne County at the courthouse in the town of Monticello On the 4th of Monday being the 28th day of January 1839

The last Will and testament of George Ewing deceased was this day produced to the Court and proven in Open Court by the Oaths of Rebekah Hayden Sarah Hayden & Micajah Phillips the three subscribing witnesses thereto in their proper persons whereupon the said Will is ordered to be recorded - And on motion of Braxton Carter & Leo Hayden the Executors named in said Will who took the Oath required by law and executed bond in the penalty of $40,000 - with John Jones & Isaac Shepperd Jr. their security conditioned as the law requires, certificate of probate is granted them in due form &c

---------------

---------------

Simon (Commonly called Si) and Juda, his wife, two negroes who were emancipated by the last will and Testament of the said George Ewing being called this day came into Court - and in pursuance to the Act of Assembly in such cases made & provided a description of of said Negroes was, by order of court, taken and is as follows, towit: -

Simon (Commonly called Si) is about 57 years old, 5 feet 9 inches & a half high, black colour, well proportioned, squarle built, and no particular accidental Marks - Juda is about 48 years old black colour, about 5 feet high, square built, well proportioned and no particular accidental marks-

Whereupon it is ordered that a certificate thereof be awarded them according to Laws And the said Negroes Simon & Juda executed Bond as is reqd. by Law each in the Penalty of $300. conditioned as the

law directs with Leo Hayden their security.

As the preceding court record indicates the slave couple Si and Juda had been emancipated in the will of their owner George Ewing. Having written his will several months earlier, George Ewing died on December 31, 1838. A copy of that will is presented here in its entirety. The reader is encouraged to read through it noting not only all references to this particular slave couple but noting as well the references made to the other slaves owned by Ewing and both the direct and subtle expressions of Ewing's feelings for those slaves. Attention should also to be given to the make up of Ewing's own family. An inventory and appraisement of George Ewing's personal estate was conducted several months after his will was probated, and a copy of that inventory is also given here.

Wayne County Wills, vol A, p.66 (Film 591.542):

I George Ewing of the County of Wayne & State of Kentucky being frail in body but of sound mind and disposing memory and considering the great uncertainty of this mortal life and the certainty of Death deem it prudent to make this my last will & testament in manner & form following, that is to say, after my decease I desire that my remains may be decently intered and grave secured by a plain Tombstone 1st I desire and direct that my Executors herein after named pay all my Just debts should any be owing at the time of my decease 2nd Item I give & bequeath to My beloved wife Elizabeth Ewing should she survive me the sum of four thousand Dollars to be paid to her by my Executors upon demand. I also give & bequeath two negroes to be chosen by her from all I may own at the time of my Death & also One bed & furniture to be selected by her self 3rd Item having been faithfully and honestly served by some of my Oldest negroes, to wit, Simon commonly called Si &

51

his wife Judah & also by one named Brown a Carpenter by trade it is my will that said negroes be sett free Simon commonly called Si & his wife Judah at my Death and Brown at my wifes Death should she survive me and if not at my Death 4th Item I do will and bequeath to the children of my deceased Daughter Polly Carter the following negroes namely Eliza the negro man Buck and also Ruth and her children. 5th Item I do will and bequeath to my Daughter Catharine P. Hayden the children of Si and his wife Judah to be possessed by my said Daughter Catharine P. Hayden during her natural life & should she have a child born of her own body that the said negroes shall descend after her Death to her child or children should she have any and if not, that is should she die childless my will is that the negroes hereby devised to her shall after the Death of my said Daughter Catharine be equally divided among & between the sons and daughters of my deceased daughter Polly otherwise called Mary Carter. 6th Item the one half of the remainder of my estate both real and personal after paying the before mentioned bequeath to my wife I bequeath and devise to my Grandchildren Sons and Daughters of my deceased daughter Polly otherwise called Mary Carter, to wit, Elizabeth E. Berry, William W. Carter, George W. Carter, Unity B. Carter, Susan M. Carter, Mary Catharine Carter and John A. Carter and to their heirs forever 7th Item it is my will and desire that my daughter Catharine P. Haydon formerly Catharine P. Ewing have the use and benefit of the other half of the remainder of my estate both real and personal not devised above during her natural life and should she have a child or children born of her Own body that this devise hereby made shall descend to her child or children after the death of my said daughter Catharine but in case my said daughter should die childless my will is that this devise and all the property or estate embraced in it shall after the Death of my said daughter Catharine P. Haydon be equally divided among the above named sons and daughters of my deceased daughter Mary Carter reserving however out of the same the sum of two thousand dollars which I will and bequeath to Leo Haydon the husband of my said Daughter Catharine provided he should survive my said daughter. It is further my will and desire that the said Leo Haydon should he survive my said daughter Catharine shall hold in addition to the two thousand dollars above named all the household & kitchen furniture heretofore given by me to my said daughter Catharine P. Haydon formerly Catharine P. Ewing 8th Item It is my will and desire that all negroes divised, by this my last will and testament, nor any one of said negroes shall ever be sold out of the Family of my children or grandchildren but that said negroes be held by my Executors for sale or distribution among legatees of this my last will and testament as said legatess may Marry or become of age & should any one of said negroes be at any time sold by either of my Executors or any one of my children or grandchildren after sale or distribution of said negroes is made among them or by any other person whatever or in any form or manner contrary to this my last will & testament my will and desire is that the negro or negroes thus sold shall by such sale become free 9th I do hereby nominate and appoint my two sons in law Braxton Carter & Leo Haydon my Executors to carry into effect this my last will & testament Signed Sealed and published this 28th day of September in the year of Our Lord One Thousand eight hundred & thirty eight

Signed sealed &          George Ewing
acknowledged in
presence of

Rebecca  X  Haden     Sarah  X  Haden
Micajah Phillips

Commonwealth of Kentucky Wayne County Court

I William Simpson Clerk of the County Court for the County aforesaid do certify that the foregoing last will & testament of George Ewing decd (which appears from the record of the Wayne County Court to have been proven at the January Court 1839 in open Court by the Oath of Rebekah Haydon Sarah Haydon and Micajah Phillips subscribing witnesses thereto) has been duly recorded in my office agreeably to an order of said County Court made pursuant to an Act entitled an Act to Authorize certain records &c of the Wayne County Court to be transcribed given under my hand this 20th June 1840

William Simpson Clk

----------------------------

Appraisements & Inventories vol. B, p.48 (Film 591,562):

The appraisement of the Slaves and personal Estate of
    George Ewing decd.
by undersigned three of the appraisers appointed by the Wayne County Court for that purpose being first duly sworn proceed as followeth, towit, [all identified as "Black"]

| | | | |
|---|---|---|---|
| Girl | Betsey sickly | age 18 yrs | $ 10 |
| Boy | John | age 10 yrs | $500 |
| Boy | George | age 7 yrs | 350 |
| Man | Buck | age 25 yrs | 800 |
| Man | Brown | age 57 carp* | 500 |
| Boy | Reuben | age 10 yrs | 550 |
| Boy | Granville | age 7 yrs | 350 |
| Boy | Isaac | age 5 yrs | 250 |
| Boy | Jacob | age 3 yrs | 150 |
| Child | Letta | age 9 mos | 100 |
| Woman | Ruth | age 31 yrs | 500 |
| Girl | Cely | age 16 yrs | 550 |
| One Rig & harness | | | 20 |

    *carpenter

Which is Most respectfully reported to the Wayne County Court July 11th 1839 - Canon Worsham, Samuel Allen & C. H. Hamilton

A comparison is made between the slaves mentioned in the will and those found listed in the inventory. The slaves Si and Juda having once been manumitted were no longer part of the Ewing estate and naturally were not included in the estate's inventory. George Ewing decreed in his will that the slaves Eliza, Buck, and the slave Ruth and her children were to be given to his grandchildren, the children of Ewing's deceased daughter Polly Carter. Buck is easily identified, and it appears that the slave identified as Eliza in the will was the slave identified on the inventory as Betsey. Considering the order in which the slaves were listed on the inventory, it is logical to speculate at least that Reuben, Granville, Isaac, Jacob and Letta were children of Ruth. No mention was made of their father, but the slave Brown would be one logical possibility. Ewing decreed that his daughter Catharine Hayden was to receive the slave children of Si and Juda. If the five children listed with Ruth were indeed hers, then John, George and Cely would have been the offspring of Si and Juda. One notes that George Ewing not only referred in his will to Si and Juda being husband and wife, but he also acknowledged Si as the father of Juda's children. Examining the slaves' appraised market values one can observe a distinct correlation between a slave's age and his/her valuation. The one blatant exception to this pattern is the slave girl Betsey.

After having located George Ewing's will, an attempt was made to chart his family. The county's marriage and vital records were used in conjunction with data from the censuses and from Cemeteries of Wayne County Kentucky to construct the following outline. It was noted that Ewing's one surviving daughter, Catherine Hayden, was herself dead by the time the estate was officially inventoried (d. June 8, 1839). According to the devise of George Ewing's will, the slaves bequeathed to Catharine also passed on to the heirs of her sister Polly Carter. Accordingly, all of the Ewing slaves except for the two chosen by Ewing's widow Elizabeth for her own personal use were inherited by the family of the Ewings' son-in-law, Braxton Carter.

Once Si was freed, documentation of his life reflected his new legal status. Having been nothing more than a statistic in the county's tax list of 1838, Si was named along with Wayne County's other free citizens on the tax list of 1839. His presence in the tax lists was followed in the ensuing years, and one can chart not only the changes in his acquisition and disposal of property but also the changes in his name. As is often the case, the tax lists, rather than answer all questions, provide the researcher with ideas for possible research in other record sources. Finding Si listed in the tax lists, first of all, informs the researcher that the former slave did not move away from the county after receiving his freedom. Finding Si listed as owning property, the researcher knows that a search of the deed books should prove fruitful. The appearance in 1853 of a George Ewing listed beside Si Ewing should not fail to pique the researcher's curiosity. The slave boy George listed in the Ewing inventory in 1839 as being seven years old, would have turned 21 years old in 1853, and if he too had somehow received his freedom, he would have appeared on the tax list that year. Appearing again on the list in 1860, this time listed as a free man of color and again listed beside Si, the assumption that George was Si's son is quite natural. Si himself appears on the county's tax lists for the last time in 1860. George appears for two more years, and then he too disappears in 1863. When the county's "colored" tax lists commenced in 1868, no blacks using either the surname Ewing or Sye (or a spelling variant of if) were found. Additional sources would need to be checked before any statements could be made concerning this disappearance of the family in the 1860's, but several initial hypotheses do come to mind: the family moved away during the upheaval of the Civil War, the adult members of the family (especially the males who would most likely be the bearers of the family name) died, or the family dropped all earlier appellations and adopted a new one. A sum-

mary of Si's listings in the tax lists are given below to illustrate the changes in his name over the years. (See Chart 16.)

Following clues provided by the tax lists, the county's deed books were searched for any pertinent entries. Several deeds were located documenting the former slave Si's purchase and sale of land. Abstracts of these deeds are given below.

Deed Book H, p. 132 (Film 590,706):

This Indenture made and entered into this 10th day of September 1839 between Martin D. Hardin of the County of Wayne and State of Kentucky of the one part and Simon Ewing a free man of color of the same County and State aforesaid of the other part Witnesseth that for and in considertion of the sum of two hundred dollars to me secured have sold and conveyed to said Simon Ewing afsd. a certain tract or parcel of land situate lying and being in the County of Wayne and State aforesaid on the waters of Cumberland River and bounded as follows towit .... together with all and singular the appertenances to the said Simon Ewing aforesaid and his heirs forever agains the claim of myself my heirs and all other persons

In Testimony whereof I here unto set my hand and seal the day and date above written
       Martin D. Hardin
acknowledged in the clerk's office by Martin D. Hardin, 10th of Sept. 1839 recorded in clerk's office, 11th day of September 1840

------------------------------

Deed Book K, p. 278 (Film 590,708):

This Indenture made this 10th day of February in the year of Our Lord 1842 between William F. McKinney and Mary his wife of the County of Wayne and State of Kentucky of the one part and Simon commonly called Sy of the County and State aforesaid of

CHART 16

## WAYNE COUNTY TAX LISTS

| | |
|---|---|
| 1839 - Ewing Sigh (col.) | 4 horses |
| 1840 - Simon Ewing of colour | 120 acres |
| 1841 - Simon Ewing of color | 130 acres Cumberland River |
| 1842 - Simon Ewing a man of color | |
| 1843 - Ewings Sye of col. | |
| 1844 - not found | |
| 1845 - Ewings Sy | 150 acres |
| 1846 - Scy Ewing (col. man) | 175 acres Sugarhollow |
| 1847 - tax book lost | |
| 1848 - Si Ewing (col. man) | 260 acres |
| 1849 - Si alias Simon man col. | 90 acres |
| listed for the first time under names beginning with 's' | |
| 1850 - Si Ewing | 93 acres |
| 1851 - Simon Ewing | |
| 1852 - not found | |
| 1853 - Ewing Si | 77 acres |
|       Ewing George | |
| 1854 - Ewin Si | 90 acres |
| 1855 - not found | |
| 1856 - not found | |
| 1857 - Ewing (Sie) | 107 acres Elk Spring Creek |
| 1858 - Sye (free man of col.) | |
| 1859 - not found | |
| 1860 - (Ewing) George free man of color | |
|       Sye (free man of col.) | |
| 1861 - Scy George | |
|       " Cyrene | |
|       " Juda | |
| 1862 - Scy, George | |
|       " Sirena | |
|       " Juda | |
| 1863 - _____ | |
| 1864 - _____ | |
| 1865 - _____ | |

the other part Witnesseth that the Said McKinney and wife for and in conideration of the sum of fifty dollars to them in hand paid the receipt whereof is hereby acknowledged have and by these presents doth grant bargain and sell unto the Sd. Simon called Sy a certain tract or parcel of land containing thirty acres...with its appertinances unto the Sd. Simon called Sy and his heirs forever,...

In testimony we have hereunto set our hands & affix our Seals the day and year first above written

William F. McKinney
Mary McKinney

---------------------------------

Deed Book J, p. 164 (Film 590,707):

5th March 1842
Rane and Sabry McKinney sell 50 acres for the sum of $150.00 to Simon, commonly called Sy. Land is located in Sugar hollow.

---------------------------------

Deed Book N, p. 618 (Film 590,709):

In consideration of the sum of Twelve Hundred and Fifty Dollars to me Sye Ewing in hand paid by George Rogers of the county of Wayne and State of Kentucky I do hereby sell and convey to him the following tract of parcel of land lying and being in the County of Wayne and State of Kentucky on the Waters of the Cumerland River in what is known and designated by the name of Sugar hollow

And bounded as follows Containing 107 acres more or less being the same land deed to me from Burrel Elam dated 23rd Sept 1853....

The title to which is hereby warranted unto said George Rogers. Witness my hand this 22nd March 1858.

Sye X Ewing

Deed Book O, p. 55 (Film 590,710):

Know all men by these presents that I Leo Hayden do hereby release all claim to a certain piece or parcel of land lying in Wayne county Kentucky in the Sugar Hollow which I held by way of Mortgage executed by Sie Ewing a free man of color...to indemnify me in the payment of a debt specified in said Mortgage recorded in the Wayne County Court Clerks Office which debt is fully paid off and discharged It is the same piece or portion of land which Scy Ewing a free man of color lately sold to George Rogers Jr. for twelve hundred dollars. Six hundred to be paid 1st of March 1858, Three hundred 1st of March 1859. And Three hundred 1st of March 1860. In witness hereof I subscribe my name and affix my seal this 1st day of April 1858.

Leo Hayden

State of Kentucky
Lincoln County

Leo Hayden personally appeared before me Champ Carter Clerk of the Lincoln County Court in my office and acknowledged the foregoing release to be his act and deed which is hereby certified to the Clerk of the Wayne County Court for record

Given under my hand &c as Clerk of Lincoln County Kentucky this 1st day of April 1858

Champ Carter Jr. D.C.

State of Kentucky Wayne County

I William Simpson Clerk of the County Court for the County Afsd. do certify that the foregoing Deed of Release from Leo Hayden to Scy Ewing a free man of Color was filed in my office for record And that the same with this certificate has been duly admitted to record. Given under my hand this 14th of May 1859

William Simpson Clk
By B. E. Roberts D.C.

Two additional deeds are presented below which are of a much more personal nature and which offer the family historian a chance to measure the character of the man called Si. George Ewing expressed concern in his will for the welfare of his slaves and stated his desire that the slaves not be sold out of the family. He decreed that any such slaves who were sold outside the family would be set free. The two deeds presented below not only serve to identify two of Si's children, but also document a father's love, sacrifice and devotion to his family. Having been freed from the bonds of slavery himself, these deeds record Si's determination to one day gain that same blessing of freedom for his children. It is not known exactly how many children Si and Juda had nor how many of those children Si was able to free. The two deeds given below are the only ones of this nature which have been found as of now. In the discussions earlier on the tax listings and on George Ewing's will, hypotheses were offered concerning the possible identities of Si and Juda's children. Some of those earlier theories are confirmed by these deeds. To the impartial genealogist merely interested in charting Si's family, the significance of these deeds though important is limited; to anyone truly interested in recovering this family's history, these deeds are treasures.

Deed Book N, p. 433 (Film 590,709):

Where as by the will of George Ewing decd. made and published on the 28th day of Sept 1838 in Wayne County Kentucky and recorded in the County Court Clerks Office for said county my son George known as George Si who was the property of the said George Ewing was to be free when ever sold out of the family of his children or Grandchildren or sold by either of his executors or any one of his children or Grandchildren And whereas said George Si was sold by a grandson-in-law of said George Ewing (Wm. Meadows) to Wm. H. Berry for my benefit at the price and sum of $600.00 which sum of money I paid for said boy George who was my son & I having been set free by the Will of said Ewing. Said money was paid & said purchase was made about the year 1848 or 9 - At said purchase I regarded my said son as free, have regarded him free ever since and now hereby so declare him to be Given under my hand this 29th day of May 1856
Attest: Shelby Stone    Si  X  Ewing


State of Kentucky
Wayne County Caourt S.S.

I William Simpson Clerk of the County Court for the county afsd. do certify that the foregoing Deed of release & Freedom from Si Ewing to George Si was on the 29th day of May 1856 produced to me in my office by the Parties and was acknowledge by the said Si Ewing to be his act and deed for the purposes therin mentioned Whereupon the same with this certificate has been duly admitted to record in my office Given under my hand this 28th day of September 1857

William Simpson Clk
By   Jno. C. Simpson DC.

The reader will want to note that although the former slave Simon (Si) was often referred to as Si Ewing, his children once freed took Si's given name as their surname.

Deed Book O, p. 159 (Film 590,710):

Whereas by the last Will and Testament of George Ewing decd. late of Wayne County Kentucky which Said Will was made and published on the 28th day of September 1838 in Wayne County Kentucky and was being duly proven and established according to law recorded in the Clerks Office of Said County. My daughter Celey known as Celey Si who was the property of the said George Ewing decd was to be free whenever sold out of the family of his children or Grandchildren or when sold by either of his Executors or any one of his children or grandchildren And whereas Said Celey Si was sold by a grandson of said George Ewing (John A. Carter) to me at the price and Sum of $750 of which Sum $650 is paid the remaining $150 I have executed to him the Said Carter my promisory note- Which Sum I have paid and obligated myself to pay for my said daughter Celey I having been set free by the Will of the said George Ewing. Said purchase of said girl Celey from said Carter was made in March 1858. At Said purchase I regarded my Said daughter Celey as free have so regarded her ever since and now hereby so declare her to be free together with her increase including her child born in April 1859 named Judy Elizabeth which said child I now do delcare free

Given under my hand this 19th day of January 1860
Att.
B. E. Roberts D.C.          Si X Ewing


Whereas my father Si Ewing has this day executed to me a Deed of release to my freedom by virtue of a devise in the last Will and Testament of George Ewing decd. now in consideration of my father's having made and acknowledged said deed And for the further consideration of the filial love and affection I entertain for him my said father. I hereby agree and bind myself to live with him and take care of him during his natural life Should I survive him

Given under my hand this 19th day of January 1860

Celey X Si


State of Kentucky
Wayne County Court C.

I B. E. Roberts Deputy Clerk for William Simpson Clerk of the County Court in and for said County of Wayne do certify that the above and foregoing Instrument of writing from Si Ewing to Celey Si and from Celey Si to Si Ewing was this day acknowl-

edged before me by them respectively to be their act and deed Wherefore I have admitted said instruments to record. Given under my hand 19th January 1860.

W. Simpson Clk
By B. E. Roberts D.C.


In an effort to learn more about the makeup of this family, a check was made of the censuses. One year after his emancipation, Si was found listed as a free head of household in the 1840 census; four others were listed as part of this household. The female listed as being between 36 and 55 years of age was obviously Si's wife Juda. The identities of the three other members of this household cannot be determined from the statistics alone, but their ages indicate they were children or young adults. The Ewings' slave named Brown was also listed in the 1840 census a free man, indicating that George Ewing's widow had decided to give the slave his freedom prior to her own death as devised in Ewing's will. Si and his wife Juda were also found in the 1850 census, but they were listed as living alone at that time. One can only speculate as to the fate of the three individuals who had been living with them ten years earlier: They had died, they moved out of the county, or possibly they were children of Si and Juda who had remained slaves but had been permitted to live with their parents while still young and were mistakenly counted in the free census in 1840. The reader will remember that the free colored in Wayne County had rather unexpectedly risen from six in 1830, to fifteen in 1840 and then dropped again to seven in 1850. (See Chart 17.)

George Ewing's widow, Elizabeth, was also listed in the 1850 census living with the family of her oldest granddaughter, Mrs. William H. Berry (the former Elizabeth E. Carter). A check of the county's probate records revealed that Mrs. Ewing died in 1857. A copy of her will and inventory of her estate are given below. Several of the slaves named in Mrs. Ewing's will were not mentioned in the probate records of her husband nineteen years earlier. One assumes that these slaves were either

58

# CHART 17

## 1840 Census

p. 178

| | | | | | | |
|---|---|---|---|---|---|---|
| Sye Ewing (colored) | Males | 1 | under 10 | Females | 1 | 10 & under 24 |
| | | 1 | 10 & under 24 | | 1 | 36 & under 55 |
| | | 1 | 55 & under 100 | | | |

Brown Brown Ewing (col.)   1  55 & under 100

*Braxton Carter, slaveowner, was listed on page 179.

---

## 1850 Census

Dist. 2, p.18

| | age | / sex | / color | / birthplace | value of real estate |
|---|---|---|---|---|---|
| Si Ewing | 71 | M | B | VA | $600 |
| Judia Sralas Ewing | 50 | F | B | VA | |

# CHART 18

## 1860 Free Census Schedule

Monticello, p.163

| | | | age | /sex | /color | /birthplace | occupation | real/personal estate |
|---|---|---|---|---|---|---|---|---|
| #1086-1075 | Celia | Sye | 35 | F | B | KY | day laborer | -/$200 |
| | Judia | " | 1 | F | B | " | | |
| | George | " | 27 | M | ·B | " | day laborer | -/$100 |
| | Betsy | " | 37 | F | B | " | idiot | |

CHART 19


<u>1810 Census</u>

George Ewing  -  3 slaves

_____


<u>1820 Census</u>

p. 93

George Ewing - slaves

Males 3  under 14        Females 4  under 14
      5  10 & under 24           2  10 & under 24
      -  24 & under 36           -  24 & under 36
      2  36 & under 55           1  36 & under 55


_____


<u>1830 Census</u>

p. 222

George Ewing - slaves

Males 2  under 10        Females 3  under 10
      5  10 & under 24           2  10 & under 24
      -  24 & under 36           -  24 & under 36
      2  36 & under 55           1  36 & under 55

offspring of older Ewing slaves, having been born in the intervening years, or were slaves which Mrs. Ewing had purchased after her husband's death. Since no bills of sale have as yet been found for such purchases, the first assumption seems the more likely. The slaves listed in Mrs. Ewing's estate inventory are of special interest since it is believed that these slaves are Si's daughter Celey and her three children. As noted earlier (Deed Book O, p. 159), Si purchased his daughter Celey's freedom in 1859. Once freed, all of Celey's children born after her manumission were likewise considered free. Her daughter, Judy Elizabeth, born in April 1859, was born a free child. Celey's three children listed in Elizabeth Ewing's inventory had been born during their mother's enslavement and remained slaves themselves even after her own emancipation. Being a free woman, Celey should have been listed in the 1860 census schedule, and such was the case.

Wayne County Wills, vol. A, p. 143 (Film 591,542):

I Elizabeth Ewing of the County of Wayne and State of Kentucky having become old and infirm but of sound mind do make this my last will and testament.

First: It is my will that all my just debts be paid. Second: I will to George W. and William W. Carter each one dollar having previously given each of them what I consider their equal and full share of my estate.

3rd having previously given Mary C. Meadows a Negro Girl by the name of Cintha valued at $600.00 and Unity B. Meadows a Negro boy by the name of John valued at $550.00 and to Elizabeth E. Berry a Negro Girl by the name of Emarine valued at $425.00 and to John A. Carter $275.00. It is my will that the three last named, viz, Unity B. Meadows, Elizabeth E. Berry and John A. Carter Shall first out of any money or property in the hands of my executor be made equal to Mary C. Meadows, the residue of my estate

both personal and real I desire shall be equally divided between Unity B. Meadows, Mary C. Meadows John A. Carter and Elizabeth E. Berry.

4th I hereby appoint William G. Meadows my sole executor of this my last will and testiment Given under my hand and seal this 25 day of March 1857

Att. J. A. Carter    Elizabeth Ewing
    Joshua Berry

Proven in Open Court November Term 1857

------------------------------

Appraisements & Inventories vol. C, p. 263 (Film 591,563):

The Inventory and Appraisement of the Estate of Elizabeth Ewing decd, which was at the Dec. Term of the Wayne County Court 1857 filed for record is in words and figures following, viz -

One Negro woman named Celey, $800. dark complected 32 or 33 yrs old
One yellow Girl named Mary Ann, $525. about 8 yrs old
One yellow complected Girl $450. about 7 yrs old & named Sarah Jane
One boy child about 18 months $225. old yellow complected named Bill

        Braxton Carter )
        Wm. Bartleson  ) Apprs.

------------------------------

Neither Si nor his wife Juda were found in the 1860 census, and one assumes that they must have died. No death record was found for them. Deed Book O, p. 159, shows that Si was alive as late as January 1860, and further hints that Juda his wife had died prior to that time since no mention was made of her. Looking at this 1860 census entry, one wonders if Betsy was not also Si and Juda's daughter. She was listed as being an "idiot," and the researcher now has an explanation for her unusually low appraisement in George Ewing's estate inventory. Since no deed of release or manumission record has been found for Betsy, one can only wonder when and how she received her freedom. Remembering the tax lists for 1861 and 1862, questions arise as to the identity of Cyrena and Juda, why these females were listed along with George, and why Celey and Betsy were not also named. With the outbreak of the Civil War, Wayne County tax lists in the first years of the war began to list all free "coloreds" both male and female. As to the identity of the female Cyrena Scy, at least two possible explanations come to mind; Cyrena was George Scy's wife, or Celey was mistakenly listed as Cyrena.

To expand one's knowledge of the slave/ex-slave Si, his family and their roots, a number of record sources remain to be investigated. The researcher will want to continue his search of the deed books for all entries involving not only the freed slaves but also George and Elizabeth Ewing and any members of their extended family. A careful survey of the Court Order Books will need to be conducted, and the researcher will want to carefully analyze the county's annual tax lists. A check of the county's surviving vital records showed a birth record for a slave boy named Bill born in June 1858, to a slave woman Celey owned by Willam H. Berry. Several additional 1850 births and deaths were recorded for Carter, Berry and Meadows' slaves, and these records can be used to help the researcher better identify the slaves listed for these owners in the 1850 and 1860 slave schedules. To better understand the makeup of Si and Juda's family, the researcher will eventually need to properly identify all slaves owned by the Ewings and their heirs. Tracking George Ewing back through the censuses, it appears that Si and Juda had been slaves of the Ewing family at least as early at 1810, and one wonders if their roots do not parallel the Ewing family's roots back into Virginia. (See Chart 19.)

Wanting to broaden our knowledge of Si's family in the post-Civil War era, a search was made of the 1870 and 1880 censuses. It is remembered that Si's son, George Si (Sye, Scy), disappeared

from the county's tax lists in 1863. No Ewings or Syes were again listed in subsequent tax lists, and no further record of George was located. Only one black citizen by the name of either Ewing or Sy was found in these post-Civil War censuses, and that single individual was Betsy Ewing. She was found in 1870 living with the family of Moses and Celia Franklin. Betsy was again classified as being an "idiot," and there can be little doubt that this was the same slave girl Betsy found in earlier records, even though there is some discrepancy in her age. She was not located in the 1880 census, and one assumes that she died during that ten-year interval.

By locating and identifying Betsy, the researcher was able to locate her sister (?) Celia. A comparison of the ages given for Celia, William and Sarah Franklin in the 1870 census with the ages given for the slaves in Mrs. Ewing's estate inventory in 1857, led to the premise that Celia Franklin and Celey Si were one and the same. No marriage record was uncovered for Moses and Celia, but it is remembered that the three children listed with Celey in the 1857 inventory were classified as yellow (Mulatto), and it is noted that whereas Celia was consistently listed as being black, Moses Franklin was mulatto. Moses and Celia were located in the 1880 census, and both census entries are given below. (See Chart 20.)

The reader will note that neither Celey's daughter Judy Elizabeth born in 1859, nor her daughter Mary Ann (listed in the 1857 inventory) born c. 1849, were listed with this family in 1870. There is a feasible gap between the ages of William and James to accommodate Judy Elizabeth. (See Chart 21.)

A deed was uncovered dated December 21, 1870, (Deed Book R, p. 164) in which Celia Franklin, "a woman of color," purchased ten acres of land from Sarah Thomas. Both women were residents of Wayne County, and Celia paid Ms. Thomas $50.00 for the land. No mention was made of either woman's husband, and no clue was given as to why Celia and Moses did not buy the land together. It is not known when Celey (Si) Franklin died,

## CHART 20

### 1870 Census

Dist. 1, Monticelo, p. 14

| | | | | | | occupation | estate real/personal | |
|---|---|---|---|---|---|---|---|---|
| #97-97 Franklin, | Moses | 49 | M | Mu | Ala | farmer | - / $125 | citizen |
| " | , Celia | 48 | F | B | KY | keeping house | | |
| " | , William | 14 | M | Mu | " | farm laborer | | |
| " | , James | 8 | M | Mu | " | at home | | |
| " | , Beldora | 4 | F | Mu | | " | | |
| " | , Permelia | 1 | F | Mu | " | " | | |
| " | , Sarah | 18 | F | Mu | " | " | | |
| Ewing | , Betsy | 60 | F | B | " | " | Idiotic | |

## CHART 21

### 1880 Census

E.D. 106, Monticello, p.22

| | | | | | | | | |
|---|---|---|---|---|---|---|---|---|
| #6-6 Franklin, | Moses | 58 | M | B | farmer | Ala | Ala | Miss |
| " | , Celia | 54 | F | B | wife | KY | VA | KY |
| " | , William | 23 | M | B | son | " | Ala | " |
| " | , James | 17 | M | B | " | " | " | " |
| " | , Beldora | 15 | F | B | dau. | " | " | " |
| " | , Amelia A. | 12 | F | B | " | " | " | " |

but the following will was recorded for her husband.

Wayne County Wills, vol. A, p. 362 (Film 591,542):

The last Will and Testament of Moses Franklin made this June 30th 1899. I Moses Franklin being of sound mind realizing that life is uncertain and death is sure and desiring to arrange my affairs in such manner as may be just and equitable as I believe to all persons, hereby make and publish this instrument as my last will and testament.

1st Having heretofore given to my oldest son William a horse, cow 7 hoges 1 ewe & lamb and 1 sow & shoats and having sheltered him with his family & fed them for nearly 1 year I feel that I have given him his just share of my labor & property and I will and bequeath to him one dollar $1.00 to be paid out of my estate

2nd I will and bequeath to my step daughter Lucinda Sallee one dollar $1.00 to be paid out of my estate

3rd I will and bequeath to John Meadows my stepson $1.00 one dollar in money to be paid out of my estate

4th I will and bequeath to Belle Franklin my daughter all my estate personal and real after the above bequeasts of one dollar each and my just debts have been paid. I desire that she shall have everything I now own and shall own at my death she having been a faithful true daughter staying with me for the past nine years and laboring for my support when all others deserted me. In the event of Belle's marriage I desire that she shall own all the property I now own inclusive and separate from her husband and any increase in the stock on the place shall belong to Lewis Franklin my grandson son of Belle

5th Having full faith in the honesty and intergrity of J. Parker Harrison I hereby appoint and name him as the executor of this my last will and testament

6th All other wills and bequests made by me heretofore I here by revoke and annul, and renounce.
This June 30th 1899
Witness            Moses X Franklin
F. R. Harrison
J. P. Harrison

Produced & Proven in Court 24th July 1899

It would appear from the bequests in Moses Franklin's will that only two of his natural children, William and Belle, survived him. His mention of stepchildren would indicate that he had at sometime remarried. No mention was made of Celia or a second wife, indicating that both had preceded him in death. Neither Belle nor her older brother William were found in the 1900 census for Wayne County, but a check of the 1900 Soundex for Kentucky revealed a William Franklin (born July 1853) who was living in Mercer County. This William Franklin had been married for sixteen years to his wife, Emma, and they were the parents of nine children, eight of whom were still living. All were natives of Kentucky as were their parents. It is not known if this was Celey's son William, but a cursory review of this census for Mercer County revealed a sizable black community in which a great number of surnames were found which were also common to blacks in Wayne County.

Following a more natural direction of genealogical investigation, an attempt was made to trace Moses Franklin back in time starting from the date of his death in 1899. The listings for Moses Franklin and his family in the 1880 and 1870 censuses have already been given above. He was found in the county's tax lists beginning with the county's first "colored" tax list in 1868. The assumption was made that Moses's choice of the surname Franklin was in someway a link to his past as a slave. A search was made of the 1860 schedule, and only one slaveowner named Franklin was found. Lewis P. Franklin was listed in the 1860 schedule as owning just one slave, a 35-year-old mulatto male. The discrepancy between this slave's age and the age given for Moses in the 1870 census was

64

small enough to encourage further research along this line. The slave's classification in both records as a mulatto was considered significant. It was also remembered that Moses Franklin's grandson named as a devisee in Moses' will was named Lewis Franklin.

Disappointment accompanied a search of the 1850 slave schedule when neither Lewis P. Franklin nor any other slaveowners by the name of Franklin were found. A search was then conducted of the 1850 free census schedule to determine if Lewis P. Franklin had been a resident of Wayne County at that time. He was located in that census, and it was learned that Lewis Franklin was only 16 years old in 1850. He was living with three young girls also named Franklin, and all four Franklin children were living with Rev. William Lockett who was 78 years old. Since the relationships between the members of a household were not stated in the 1850 census, Lewis Franklin's relationship to William Lockett could only be guessed at--it was conjectured that William Lockett was the Franklin children's grandfather.

A search was again made of the 1850 slave schedule, and a listing was found for William Lockett. Only one slave was listed for him, a 25-year-old mulatto male. Once again the data given for this slave seemed to correspond with the information available for Moses.

A cursory review of the county's tax lists provided the researcher with additional clues and information. The 1855 tax schedule showed Lewis Franklin, as the representative of the heirs of E. Franklin, owning one adult slave appraised at the market value of $650.00. This was the first such listing for Lewis Franklin, and it coincided with his turning 21. William Lockett was found listed as the representative of the Franklin heirs in 1852 and 1853, and he was also listed as owning one adult slave (valued at $700.00 in 1853, and $600.00 in 1852). A search of earlier tax lists showed an Elisha Franklin in 1839, owning one slave under the age of 16. Franklin was not found in the lists in the 1840's, and one wonders if he perhaps did not live for a period of time outside the county. A marriage record was found for Elisha Franklin and Elizabeth Lockett, daughter of William Lockett, dated 1826.

A search of the probate records produced a copy of William Lockett's will written in January 1850, and proven May 23, 1853 (Wayne County Wills, vol. A, p. 129). Lockett's will confirmed the earlier hypothesis that Lewis Franklin and his sisters were William Lockett's grandchildren. No slaves were mentioned in Lockett's will, but the evidence already mentioned from the other record sources indicated that the Franklin heirs inherited their slave from their father rather than from their Lockett grandfather.

All evidence seems to indicate that the slave Moses had been owned by members of the Franklin family for a number of years. A more extensive investigation of all records pertaining to the Franklin family would certainly prove to be productive. Evidence has been found placing Elisha Franklin in Wayne County at least as early as 1813 (Deed Book B, p. 104). Moses claimed to have been born in the state of Alabama, and these two facts seem to imply that the slave boy, Moses, was purchased by the Franklin family sometime after his birth. A careful review of the deed books and court records should produce a bill of sale and a record of Moses' importation into the state. The possibility of Moses' parents, or at least his mother, having also been brought to the county should not be overlooked.

An outline of Si's family and Moses Franklin's ties to it is given as an accompaniment to this report. Many names are missing, and many questions remain unanswered. As stated earlier, the preceding reports do not claim to be completed family histories formulated from an exhaustive investigation of all possible record sources. It is hoped that one of the principal by-products of these case studies will be to serve as a catalyst to pique the researcher's curiosity and imagination, and these studies will inspire the prospective family historian to chart his or her own course of investigation in pursuit of those missing links and unanswered questions.

## GENEALOGY OF THE EWING FAMILY (SLAVE OWNERS)

```
                  George Ewing = Elizabeth Wallace
                  1769-1838    |   1777-1857
                               |
          -------------------------------------------------
          |                                          |
  Mary "Polly" = m 1817 Braxton Carter*    Catharine P. = m 1833 Leo Haydon
  1798-1837    |        1798-1863           1810-1839    |
               |                                         |
               |                                      no issue
               |
```

Elizabeth E. Carter  (1817-1911) m. 1837, William H. Berry   (1813-1864)
Willlam W. Carter    (1820-   ) m.     , Mary Metcalf
George W. Carter     (        ) m. 1846, Theresa Van Winkle
Unity BatesCarter    (1825-1864) m. 1842, James H. Meadows   (1818-    )
Susan M. Carter      (1829-1852)         unmarried
Mary C. Carter       (1831-   ) m. 1848, William G. Meadows (1826-   )
John A. Carter       (1835-   ) m. 1858, Margaret Bobbitt

* Braxton Carter m. 2nd, 1839, Mrs. Burnetta (Thomas) Taylor (1817-1853)
  and had 4 children: Eliza, Harrison, Charles, Angaletta.  He m. 3rd,
  1859, Eleanor Chaplin.


## GENEALOGY OF THE SLAVE SIMON, COMMONLY CALLED SI

```
                  Si (Ewing)  =  Juda (Ewing)
                  1779/81-1860 | 1790/1800-185_
                  freed 1839   |  freed 1839
                               |
    ----------------------------------------------------------------------
    |        |           |                      |         |          |
    ?      Betsey      Celey Si  =  Moses Franklin*    John    George Si   ?
         c1821-187_    1823/25-18__|  1821/25-1899    c1829-   1832-
         freed before 1860  freed 1858|                         freed
                               |                                1848/56
                               |
    ----------------------------------------------------------------------
    |          |           |          |           |         |          |
 Mary Ann  Sarah Jane  William   Judy Elizabeth  James   Beldora "Belle"  Amelia A.
 1849-       1851-     1856-19__   1859-186_      1862-    1865-19__       1868-
 (b slave) (b slave)  (b slave)   (b free)      (b free)    |
                      m. (Emma?)                            |
                      children:                       Lewis Franklin
                                                      18__ - 19__
```

* John Meadows & Lucinda Sallee were step-children of Moses Franklin

66

The desirability and need for more extensive investigations into the lives of slaves who were located on small farms and in small towns, as opposed to those slaves located on large plantations, and the benefits derived from such investigations for social as well as family historians have been discussed in the introduction of this study. Subsequent chapters have mentioned the inherent problems involved in research along these lines, and a survey has been presented of pertinent research sources and techniques. The special problems facing any student of slave ancestry have been highlighted with accompanying explanations on the most logical methods for arriving at their solutions. The case studies presented in this final chapter have converted theoretical situations into actual practice, and the range and variety of information that can be extracted on slave families from an assortment of traditional and untraditional sources has been explored. By utilizing the information presented in this study, it is hoped that other historians will see the practicality of researching slave ancestry and the wealth of information that can be gained from such investigations.

## ENDNOTES

1. Eugene D. Genovese, <u>Roll Jordon Roll: The World The Slaves Made</u> (New York: Vintage Books, 1976), p. 7.

2. Robert W. Fogel and Stanley L. Engerman, <u>Time on the Cross: The Economics of Slavery</u> (Boston: Little, Brown & Co., 1974); Edwin Adams Davis, ed., <u>Plantation Life in the Florida Parishes of Louisiana, 1836-1846, as Reflected in the Diary of Bennet H. Barrow</u> (New York: 1943); and Herbert G. Gutman, <u>Slavery and the Numbers Game: A Critique of Time On the Cross</u> (Chicago: University of Illinois Press, 1975) p.17.

3. Herbert G. Gutman, <u>The Black Family In Slavery And Freedom, 1750-1925</u> (New York: Pantheon Books, 1976).

4. Ibid., p. 102.

5. Genovese, p. 5.

6. Frederick Douglass, <u>Life and Times of Frederick Douglass</u> (Hartford, Conn.: Park Publishing Co., 1881), p. 26.

7. E. Kay Kirkham, <u>A Survey of American Census Schedules</u>, 2nd ed. (Provo, Utah: Stevenson's Genealogical Center, 1972); "Census Records," <u>Guide to Genealogical Research in the National Archives</u> (Washington, D.C.: National Archives and Records Service, 1982):9-38.

8. Herbert G. Gutman, <u>The Black Family In Slavery and Freedom, 1750-1925,</u> (New York: Pantheon Books, 1976), pp. 230-256; and Eugene D. Genovese, <u>Roll Jordan Roll</u> (New York: Vintage Books, 1976), pp. 445-447.

9. <u>Bluegrass Roots</u>, vol. X, no. 2 (Summer 1983), p. 64.

10. <u>1810-1900 U. S. Population Censuses</u>, Wayne County, Kentucky; and <u>1850-1860 U. S. Slave Schedule Censuses</u>, Wayne County, Kentucky.

11. C. Stewart Boertman, <u>The Sequence of the Occupance In Wayne County, Kentucky: An Historical Study</u> (Ph.D. dissertation, University of Michigan, 1934).

12. Wayne County, Kentucky <u>Deed Book A</u>, p. 118 (LDS Genealogical Society Library: Film 509,703).

13. Ivan E. McDougle, <u>Slavery In Kentucky</u> (Clark University: Ph.D. dissertation, 1918; reprint ed., Westport, Conn.: Negro Univ. Press, 1970), p. 76.

14. Clarence L. Mohr, "Slavery in Oglethorpe County, Georgia," <u>Phylon</u> 33 (Spring 1972):12.

15. Charles S. Sydnor, <u>Slavery In Mississippi</u> (1933; reprint ed., New York: American Historical Association, 1965), p. 133.

16. Wayne County, Kentucky <u>Deed Book B</u>, p. 108-109 (LDS Genealogical Society Library: Film 590,703).

17. Frederic Bancroft, <u>Slave-Trading In The Old South</u> (Baltimore: Furst Co., 1931), p. 147.

18. <u>Deed Book A</u>, p. 106.

19. Wayne County, Kentucky <u>Appraisements & Inventories</u>, p. 288 (LDS Genealogical Society Library: Film 591,562).

20. Deed Book A, p. 133.

21. Wayne County, Kentucky Deed Book D, p. 415 (LDS Genealogical Society Library: Film 590,704).

22. McDougle, Slavery in Kentucky, p. 46.

23. Deed Book D, p. 314.

24. McDougle, Slavery in Kentucky, p. 65.

25. Ibid., p. 116.

26. Wayne County, Kentucky Court Order Book A, p. 32 (LDS Genealogical Society Library: Film 591,543).

27. Wayne County, Kentucky Court Order Book G, p. 30 (LDS Genealogical Society Library: Film 591,545).

28. Court Order Book G, p. 74.

29. Wayne County, Kentucky Court Order Book D, p. 35 (LDS Genealogical Society Library: Film 591,544).

30. Wayne County, Kentucky Court Order Book E, p. 45 (LDS Genealogical Society Library: Film 591.544).

31. Court Order Book G, p. 111.

32. Ibid., p. 122.

33. Wayne County, Kentucky Court Order Book F, p. 247 (LDS Genealogical Society Library: Film 591,545).

34. Wayne County, Kentucky Court Order Book K, p. 331 (LDS Genealogical Society Library: Film 591,547).

35. Wayne County, Kentucky Tax Books, 1863-1865 (LDS Genealogical Society Library: Film 008,272).

36. 1860 U. S. Population Census, Wayne County, Kentucky.

37. Wayne County, Kentucky Tax Books, 1868-1870 (LDS Genealogical Society Library: Film 008,272 - 008, 273).

38. Ibid.

39. Genovese, Roll Jordan Roll, p. xvii.

40. Jacqueline Coffey Sexton, The Coffeys of Wayne County (Monticello, Ky.: By the Author, 1974).

41. Will Frank Steely, "The Established Churches and Slavery, 1850-1860," The Register of the Kentucky Historical Society 55 (April 1957):98.

42. Ala Shearer Vickery and Elizabeth Simpson, Deeds and Records Pertaining to Shearer Valley Church of Christ (Monticello, Ky.: By the Authors, 1975, p. 15.

43. August Phillips Johnson, A Century of Wayne County, Kentucky, 1800-1900 (Louisville: Standard Printing Co., 1939), p. 83.

44. Garnet Walker, Pleasant Vineyards (Monticello, Ky.: By the Author, 1960), p. 7 (LDS Genealogical Society Library: Film 728,097, item 9).

45. Will Frank Steely, "The Established Churches and Slavery, 1850-1860," The Register of the Kentucky Historical Society 55 (April 1957); and Gaston Hugh Wamble, "Negroes and the Missouri Protestant Churches Before and After the Civil War," Missouri Historical Review 61 (April 1967):321-347.

46. Ray Allen Billington and Martin Ridge, Westward Expansion, 5th ed. (New York: MacMillan Publishing Co., 1982).

47. Elaine C. Everly, "Marriage Registers of Freedmen," Prologue: Journal of the National Archives 5 (Fall 1973):150-154.

48. "Records of Black Americans," Guide to Genealogical Research in the National Archives (Washington, D.C.: National Archives and Records Service, 1982 171-185.

49. List of Black Servicemen Compiled from the War Department Collection of Revolutionary War Records (Washington,

D.C.: National Archives and Records Service, 1978).

50. John David Smith, "The Recruitment of Negro Soldiers In Kentucky, 1863-1865," The Register of the Kentucky Historical Society 72 (October 1974):364-390.

51. Biographical information concerning the families mentioned in these case studies has been gathered from the appropriate census records and from the following sources: June Baldwin Bork, Wayne County, Kentucky: Vital Records, 3 vols. (Huntington Beach, Calif.: By the Author, 1973); Bennie Coffey, Cemeteries of Wayne County Kentucky (Monticello, Ky: Lakeview Printing, Inc., 1982); and Augusta Phillips Johnson, A Century of Wayne County, Kentucky, 1800-1900 (Louisville: Standard Printing Co., 1939).

52. Ibid.

53. 1900 U. S. Population Census, Wayne County, Kentucky, E. D. 131.

# APPENDICES

## Appendix A: Probate Records

Will of Lewis Russell Coffey,* 1850 (abstracted)

In the name of God amen I Lewis Coffey of the County of Wayne being sick and weak in boddy but of sound mind and disposing memory (for which I Thank God) and calling to mind the uncertainty of human life as it has pleased God to bless me with I give and bequeath the same in manner following that is to say after the payment of all my just debts and funeral expenses
First

I give to my beloved wife Biddy Coffey the following slaves (towit) Agnes and all her Children now with her, Sarah and her children and Nancy. Subject to her own controll, disposal, sale or devise in any such way and manner as may be most agreeable to her own feelings
Secondly

I give to my beloved wife Biddy Coffey my Black man Charles, my slave Jane & Bill during her natural life
Thirdly

I give to my beloved wife Biddy Coffey the farm I now live upon and all adjoining land during her natural life
Fourthly

I give six hundred Dollars out of my Estate to each one of the following named of my children Betsy Rachel Polly James Henderson Shelby Benjamin F. and Thomas to make them equal in amount with what my son E.N.C. Coffey has heretofore received....
Twelfthly

My Black Woman Cass is to remain in the possession of my wife during the natural life of my wife should said black woman live so long at the death of my wife to be by my executors taken care of and ample provisions out of my estate by them made for her support whilst she may live provided she may not be able comfortably to support herself....
Fourteenthly

My will and desire is after the death of my wife that all the rest of my estate undisposed of by her both real and personal of whatever nature or kind soever it may be-- be by my executors sold...equally divided among the following of my children (towit) Betsy, Rachel, Polly, James, Henderson, Shelby, Benjamin F and Thomas C

I do hereby Constitute and appoint Henderson B. F. Coffey and Shelby Coffey executors of this my Last Will and Testament and the County Court upon their taking Oath as executors are not required to bind them to security for the execution of this my last Will

In Testimony whereof I have hereunto set my hand this 13th Day of April 1850

Witness                          Lewis Coffey
Joshua Buster
Wm Simpson

*Jacqueline Coffey Sexton, The Coffeys of Wayne County (Monticello, Ky.: By the Author 1974), pp. 42-45

------------------------------

Wills (Film 591,542*)

p. 135 Will of William Gillespie (abstracted)

73

First I give to my wife, Nancy Gillespie, the following negro slaves Perry & Rebecca his wife, Isaac and William, Rebecca's children; also Rose and Louis her child, and Lucinda and Green her child.

At the termination of the above devise, by death or otherwise It is my will that the above Land & Negroes be equally divided among my sons and daughters It is further my will that the Negroes now in the possession of Nancy Cowan, my motherinlaw be and remain with her during her natural life and at her death I desire that David Rankin and Saml Gover my sons in law receive out of sd Negroes one Negro each at their appraised value, and the ballance of the children to be made equals as they become of age in a negro & property

It is further my will that the negroes above named now in the possession of Nancy Cowan my mother in law at her death all fall into the hands of my Executors and become assetts in their hands to be managed by my executors to the best advantage for the Estate. Regarding sd Negroes comfort & well being It is further my will that all the Negroes belonging to me be kept in the Family as long as they behave well. And if any should become Refractory and ungovernable then it shall be the duty of my Executors to hire such Refractory Slaves for the best price that can be had until they make amends.

It is further my will that all property belonging to me and not otherwise dispossed of Shall be assetts in the hands of my Executors: to be managed and dispossed of as they think proper for the use of my heirs. It is my will that all my children in the final distribution receive an equal portion of my estate. I hereby appoint Samuel Gover & David Rankin my Executors to carry into affect this my last Will and Testament

Given under my hand this 13th day of Dec in the year of Christ 1854

Proved in Court              Wm Gillespie
Feb Term 1855

*Film numbers refer to microfilm copies of original records. Films can be found at the LDS Genealogical Society Library in Salt Lake City, Utah.

------------------------------

Appraisements & Inventories, 1852-1889 (Film 591,563)

p. 211 Inventory and Appraisement of the Estate of William Gillespie, 1855

| man | Perry | $900 | boy | Lewis | $200 |
|-----|-------|------|------|---------|------|
| boy | William | $800 | woman | Rebecca | $700 |
| boy | Isaac | $500 | woman | Rose | $700 |
| boy | Green | $500 | woman | Lucinda | $700 |

------------------------------

Wills  (Film 591,542) (abstracted)

pp. 53-54  Sept. 9, 1833 Will of Samuel Copenhaver

Samuel Copenhaver gave his wife Viana her choice of three or four of the Negroes from the Estate. Viana and Samuel's son Thomas Copenhaver were named executors.

------------------------------

Appraisements & Inventories, 1816-1853 (Film 591,562)

p. 350 Appraisement & Inventory of the Estate of Samuel Copenhaver, Nov. 1835

Lavina & Thomas Copenhaver, Executors

| woman | Nana | $550 | boy | Tomda | $500 |
|-------|------|------|------|-----------|------|
| " | Patsy | $575 | girl | Lucinda | $375 |
| " | Eliza | $375 | " | Polly Ann | $250 |
| " | Barbara | $575 | " | Amanda | $125 |
| " | Lydda | $550 | " | Everline | $150 |
| man | George | $800 | boy | Perry | $150 |

*Notice the variances in estimated market values. This normally reflected differences in the slaves' ages and sex. A comparison with those slaves named Copenhaver in the 1870 Census, indicates that the man George was about 19 years old at the time of this inventory and the boy Perry was about three.

Samuel Copenhaver was listed owning the

following slaves in the 1830 Census:

males: 1 under 10
1 10 & under 24

females: 1 under 10
4 10 & under 24
1 24 & under 36

Lavina Copenhaver had the following slaves listed in the 1840 Census:

males: 3 under 10
1 24 & under 36

females: 3 under 10
2 10 & under 24
2 24 & under 36

Lavina Copenhaver had 12 slaves in the 1850 Slave Schedule and 27 in 1860.

Thomas Copenhaver had 6 slaves in the 1850 Slave Schedule and 11 in 1860.

Lavina Copenhaver died in 1871, thus, no mention of slaves would appear in her Will.

------------------------------

Will abstracts  (Film 591,542)

p. 117   Will of Allen Weaver 18 Sept. 1850

to daughter, Susan Mary Jewel a negro girl named Sarah
to son, Elijah Weaver a negro boy named Walker
to daughter, Margaret Ann a negro girl named Cela
to son, William Weaver a negro boy named Woodson
to son, Mason Allen Weaver a negro boy named Strander
to son, James F. Weaver a negro boy named William
to son, Sherman T. Weaver a negro boy named John Phillip

------------------------------

p. 125   Will of James Sloan 11 November 1846

to my granddaughter, Martha Frances Thompson Sloan, a negro girl Cleary; requests that the rest of the negroes be sold within the family.

------------------------------

p. 162   Will of Elizabeth Chesney 30 November 1858

After all my Just debts and funneral expenses are paid I wish the following disposition made of the property of which I may die possessed...
In the next place I give to my Brother Jno. Rousseau and his heirs my negro man Dick according to the power vested in me by the Will of my father James Rousseau decd.

------------------------------

Appraisements & Inventories
(Film 591,562)

p. 100   Inventory of the Estate of Joseph Hinds, 1820

one negro woman named Caty
  about the age of 35 years
  and four children: Allen,
  Austin, Patience & Esther         $1,100
One negro man named Jim             $ 500
one negro man named Daniel          $ 375
one negro boy named Squire          $ 375
one negro woman named Suke
  & mulatto child Hamilton          $ 500

------------------------------

Apraisements & Inventories, 1816-1853
(Film 591,562)

p. 1   An Inventory of the Estate of A. Gholson, Feb. 1816

one old negro man Sims
one old negro woman Hannah
one old negro woman Lucy and child Tom
one negro girl Mariah
one negro boy Thornton
one negro boy Jack
one boy Green
one yellow girl Carolina
one boy Mark
one yellow boy Edmund

list of Sales of the Estate of A. Gholson, 21 & 22 of March 1816

Benj Gholson
   Hired one Boy called Edmund  $28.12
Barth Haden  Hired old Si  $30.00
John Gholson one boy called Mark  $39.00
James Gholson one boy called Jack  $24.00
John Gholson one boy called Green  $25.50
Samuel Gholson
   Hired one negro girl Caroline  $35.00
Barth haden  Hired Hannah  $10.00
Samuel Gholson & John Gholson
   One Family of Negroes called
   Lucy, Riah, Thornton, Thomas  $16.00

-----------------------------

p. 64 Inventory of the Estate of Michael Stoner, 1814

| | | |
|---|---|---|
| negro man | Joe | $200 |
| negro woman | Sally | $250 |
| negro woman | Priscilla | $300 |
| negro boy | Walker | $375 |
| negro boy | Uriah | $375 |
| negro boy | Miley | $375 |
| negro girl | Dicey | $300 |
| negro boy | Abram | $375 |
| negro boy | Anthony | $300 |
| negro girl | Angess | $275 |
| negro girl | Mary | $250 |
| negro boy | Aquilla | $250 |
| negro girl | Mahala | $175 |
| negro girl | Lucy Ann | $175 |
| negro boy | Brown | $125 |
| negro boy | London | $125 |

p. 286 Inventory of the Estate of Ambrose Weaver, 16 October 1836

| | | |
|---|---|---|
| one negro man | Nelson | $450 |
| one negro man | Walker | $450 |
| one negro woman | Polly | $300 |
| one negro woman | Ann | $300 |
| one negro boy | Joseph | $150 |
| one negro boy | Bennoni | $100 |
| one negro girl | Malinda | $100 |

-----------------------------

Appraisements & Inventories, 1816-1853 (Film 591,562)
p. 288 Sale of the Estate of Ambrose Weaver, October 1836

James Weaver
   for the hire of Walker  1 month $5.37
Wm. Hitchison
   for the hire of Nelson  1 month $6.00
Allen Weaver
   for the hire of Ann  1 month $1.43

James Weaver  buys Walker  $472.87
James Ford  buys Nelson  $450.50
Wm. Hutchison buys Polly & Child $453.00
"   "   buys Joseph  $100.00
"   "   "  Bennoni  $ 90.00
Allen Weaver  Buys Ann  $402.50
"   "   "  Malinda Jane $100.37

*Legal Heirs of Ambrose Weaver:

  James Weaver, Allen Weaver, Elijah Weaver, Lucy (Mrs. James Ford), Susan (Mrs. Wm. Hutchison), and Catharine (Mrs. John F. Barker).

## Appendix B: Deed Abstracts

### Bills of Sale

Deed Book A, p. 42 (Film 590,703)

Know all men by these present that I William Beard of the County of Wain & Stat of Kentucky hath bargained, sold confirmed & deleivered unto James Skuggs of the County of Wain & State above mentioned a Negroe Girl of the name of Mary aged eleven years & I do by these presents warren & forever defend right of the above named Negro from me & my airs to the above named James Skuggs & his airs & all other rights, claimes or demanes for a valueable consideration of Ninety pounds to me in hand paid before sealing & deleivering of these present As witness my hand & Seal this 9th of July 1802
Test

   Reuben Sl_____      Wm Beard

Deed Book B, p. 223 (Film 590,703)

Know all men by these presents that Jeremiah Burnett of Wayne County and State of Kentucky doth make over and confirm unto Isaac Burnett of the County and State aforesaid one Negro boy by the name of Adam for and in consideration of the said Isaac Burnett paying the said Jeremiah Burnett the sum of four hundred Dollars and the said Jeremiah Burnett doth forever warrant and defend the said boy Adam unto the said Isaac Burnett his heirs and assigns forever. In witness whereof I have hereunto set my hand and seal this ninth day of March one thousand Eight hundred and fifteen. Teste

          John Hurt          Jeremiah Burnett
          Joseph Hurt
          William Sloan
          James Hurt

--------------------------------

Deed Book L, p. 268 (Film 590,708)

Know all men by these presents that we Aaron Wolsey and Elizabeth Woolsey his wife of the County of Wayne and State of Kentucky of the one part and Thomas Copenhaver of the County and State of afsd of the other part witnesseth that the Said Woolsey & wife for and in consideration of the Sum of Five hundred dollars to them in hand paid the receipt of which is hereby acknowledged have this day granted bargained and Sold and by these presents doth grant bargain Sell transfer and convey unto the Said Thomas Copenhaver his heirs and assigns our undivided interst being one half in and to four certain nergroes all of which are now in the possession of Sd Copenhaver, One a Negro girl named Milly aged 30 years of a black color and her three children towit. James aged about eight years Tom aged about Six years Amy Elizabeth aged about four years of a black color the said Milly being the same Negro girl given to the said Elizabeth Woolsey formerly of Elizabeth Copenhaver and Catharine Copenhaver by deed of gift of record in the Clerks office of the Wayne County Court having date 25th Sept 1843. To

have and to hold the undivided interest aforesaid in and to the afsd, negros unto sd, Copenhaver and his heirs the right title interest and claim to Sd Negros we the party of the first do & will forever warrant and defend against the claim of themselves their heirs and against the claim or claims of all every other person or persons whomsoever In testimony whereof we have hereunto Set our names and affixed their Seals this 10th day of March 1851.

          A. T. Woolsey
          Elizabeth Woolsey

*Compare with Deed of Gift, Deed Book I, p. 64

--------------------------------

Deed Book B, p. 104 (Film 590,703) (abstract)

Elisha Franklin sold to William and Nancy Franklin a negro woman named Betty aged 18 years old, for the sum of $300.00.   1813

## Deeds of Gift

Deed Book I, p. 64 (Film 590,707)

Know all men by these presents that I Christopher Simpson of the County of Wayne and State of Kentucky have this day for and in Consideration of the love and affection that I have for my two granddaughters Catharine & Elizabeth Copenhaver of the aforesaid County & State and as an advancement to them and the heirs of their bodys given granted and conveyed to them and to the heirs of their bodys the Said two granddaughters Catharine Copenhaver and Elizabeth Copenhaver and the heirs of their bodys a certain Negro girl Slave named Milly about sixteen years of age Also her negro child by the name of James about ten months of age which said Negros is to be equally divided Between my Said two Granddaughters when the younger one towit Elizabeth Copenhaver arrives at lawful age which Said Negores my said

Granddaughters is to have and to hold to them and the heirs of their bodys forever

In Testimony whereof I have hereunto Set my hand and Seal this 25th of Septr 1843
Test
Michael Castillo     Christopher Simpson
S. D. Hutchison

------------------------------

Deed Book B, p. 112 (Film 590,703)

Know all men by these presents that I Jeremiah Burnett of Wayne County and State of Kentucky for many good causes and divers considerations and the great love and affection I have to my Son in law James Hurt do give and bequeath and by these presents doth make over and confirm unto him the said Hurt to him his heirs & assigns forever one negro Girl Sarah about Six years old with all her Increase or profits that may arise or in any wise arise from the said negro likewise ninety acres of land by the same more or less whereon the said Hurt now lives being part of the said tract wherein I now live having such Temporary lines as agreed on between the parties herein mentioned together with all any Singular the right members and appurtenances thereunto belonging or in any wise appertaining with every aprt and parcel therof and I the said Jeremiah Burnett for myself my heirs and every other person and persons whatsoever doth forever warrant and defend the said mentioned property unto the said James Hurt his heirs and assigns forever and doth post the said Hurt in full possession of the same at the Signing and delivery of these presents In Witness whereof I have hereunto set my hand and Seal this fourteenth day of October One Thousand Eight hundred and Twelve Signed Sealed & delivered
In presence of
John Parrish     Jeremiah (X) Burnett
Benjamin Denny

------------------------------

Deed Book O, p. 33 (Film 590,710)

To all to whom these presents shall come greeting know ye that I Francis Redman of the County of Fentress and State of Tennessee for and in consideration of the natural love and affection which I have for my daughter Pollyan Burnette of Wayne county Kentucky and for the further consideration of the Sum of One Dollar to me in hand paid at and Before and delivery of these presents the receipt of which I do hereby acknowledge have given and granted and by these presents do give and grant unto the Said Pollyan Burnette and Jonathan Burnette her husband a certain Negro girl now in the possession of Said Burnette named Serrena aged about eleven years old to have and to hold the Said negro girl Serrena to them and Said Polly and Jonathan Burnette and their heirs &c forever and furthermore I will warrant and defend the title to Said Negro girl to them the Said Jonathan and Pollyan Burnette their heirs &c against the lawful claim or demand of all presents forever I witness whereof I have hereunto Set my hand and Seal this the 13th day of August 1858
Test
Absolam Miller     Francis Redman
Harrison Williams

State of Kentucky
Wayne County Court S.S.

I Wm Simpson Clerk of the county court for the county afsd, do certify that this deed of Gift from Francis Redman to Jonathan Burnette & Pollyan his wife was on the 13th of Octr. 1858 produced to me and proven by the Oaths of Absolam Miller and Harrison Williams subscribing witnesses to the act and deed of the said Francis Redman whereupon the same together with this certificate have been duly admitted to record in my office Given under my hand this 19th day of Feb. 1859
Wm. Simpson Clk
By J. E. Wright Dclk

------------------------------

Deed Book J, p. 440 (Film 590,707)
(abstract)

Francis Redman of Fentress County, Tennessee gave to his daughter Elizabeth B. Chrisman, wife of William C. Chrisman, of Wayne county, Kentucky, a negro boy named Andy, five years old. 12 April 1845

*Although Francis Redman was a resident of Fentress County, Tennessee, this deed was recorded in the deed books of Wayne County, Kentucky where William and Elizabeth Chrisman were residents. It is possible that a copy of this deed of gift was also filed in the deed books of Fentress County.

## Mortgage Deeds

Deed Book A, p. 133 (Film 590,703)

Know all men by these presents that I William Beard of the County of Wayne & State of Kentucky have this 8th day of April 1805 bargained sold & delivered & by these presents do bargain, sell & deliver to Christopher Catrine a Negro boy about Eight years of age which boy I bind myself, my Heirs &c to defend against the claim of all & every person whatsoever The Condition of the above bill of Sale is this That if the above bound William Beard doth return unto the said Christopher Catrine the sum of Ł 47--2-0 which the said Beard has now borrowed within three months with Interest from the date hereof the above Christopher Catrine is to redeliver the said Negro boy unto the said William Beard Given under my hand & Seal the day & date above written
Teste                              Wm Beard
Tunstall Quarles Junr
George Hammond
Roger Oatts

---

Deed Book E, p. 346 (Film 590,705)

Whereas Gorden C. Stephens of the County of Wayne & State of Kentucky hath this day for and in consideration of the Sum of $1500 current money to him in hand

paid or secured to be paid by the Said Worshan Granted bargained and Sold unto the Said Worsham and his heirs forever three sertain Negroes viz Barberry & her two children named Neely and Edmund & do by these present warrant and forever defend the right and title to the Said Negroes to the Said Canan Worsham against the claim of himself his heirs &c and against the claim or claims of all and every other pers or persons whomsoever Subject to the following Condition towit whereas the Said Cannan Worsham is bound as Security for Said Stephens in an Obligation Executed to T. & E. Hutchison in which obligation they are bound to pay unto Said Hutchisons the amount of a note executed to Said Stephens by William Green dated the 24th day of November 1831 for the Sum of $1000 and assigned to Said Hutchisons by G, C, Stephens
If the said William Green becomes insolvent So that the amount of Said Note cannot be made of his estate or otherwise shall fail to pay and discharge said Note on or before the 24th day of November 1831 If therefore the Said Note shall will and truly be discharged with its interest & cost or the Said Cannan Worsham be released from all liability as Security for Said Stephens in said Obligation on or before the afsd 24th day of November 1831 then the foregoing conveyance to be void else to remain in full force this 29th day of March 1831
                        Gorden C. Stepehens

---

Deed Book D, p. 415 (Film 590,704) (abstract)

John Shoemate had three slaves returned to him whom he had earlier mortgaged out to Robert M. Smith. The slaves were named: Liberty, Anna, and Sharlott. 1828

## Records of Importations

Deed Book D, p. 314 (Film 590,704)

State of Kentucky  Wayne County

This day personally appeared before me B. Hadon a Justice of the Peace for Wayne County Joshua Buster a Citizen of Wayne County Kentucky and made oath that he purchased a negro slave a female by the name of Sally which slave he purchased in the State of Tennessee and County of Fentriss and brought into this State for his own use and without any intention of selling her again
Given under my hand this 19th of March 1827

B. Hadon  J.P.

-----------------------------------

Deed Book D, p. 314

I do certify that Rolen Burnet came this day before me Ransom Vanwinkle a Justice of the peace for Wayne county Kentucky and made oath that he had brought five negores to the state of Kentucky for his own service and that he did not bring them with the intention of selling them and their names is Sivey Stephen Stephen David and Mary
Given under my hand this 22nd Day of February 1827

Ransom Vanwinkle

-----------------------------------

Deed Book D, p. 420

February 9th 1828 This day came Nimrod Ingram before the undersigned Justic of the peace and made oath that he has brought in some negroes to this state for his own use and not to sell in this state and by the name of Gabriel, Judy Mary Martha Malindy Robert Marier Mary & Catherine

Lewis Coffey  J. P.

-----------------------------------

Deed Book D, p. 418
(abstract)

Joshua Buster appeared before B. Hadon a Justice of the Peace on the 3rd of March 1828 to acknowledge buying two slaves in Tennessee and bringing them into Wayne county Kentucky for his own use and not to sell. The slaves were named Lewis & Spencer.


Manumission Certificates


Deed Book I, p. 55 (Film 590,707)

Know all men by these presents that I Joshua Buster of the County of Wayne Ky in consideration of the Sum of five hundred dollars part of which is paid and part to be paid and of the kind and benevolent feelings that I have for Garret who has heretofore served me well, do hereby forever manumit and set him (garret) free - and declare it as my intention and wish and declare it as the intention of this writing that he shall enjoy as full and perfect freedom as if he had been born free - hereby releasing him from the obligations of Slavery and Servitude forever
In Testimony whereof I hereunto Set my hand & Seal this the 27th day of February 1845
Attest                          Joshua Buster
  S. Beard
  J. B. Collins

State of Kentucky Wayne County Court Set March Court 1845

I William Simpson Clerk of the County Court for the County Afsd do hereby certify that the foregoing deed of emancipation from Joshua Buster to his Servant Garret, has been duly recorded in my office
Given under my hand this 6th day of December 1845

William Simpson CWC

-----------------------------------

Deed Book B, p. 406 (Film 590,703)

To all whom it may concern be It Known that I James Walker of the County of Wayne and State of Kentucky for divers good caus and considerations thereunto moving as, also in further Consideration of Taking a farm of 20 acres on my land

and using all incentry for a living and to pay me the Half what he can make fourteen years, also to pay his own taxes and fence himself and if need requires In the winter season to assist me in getting wood and feeding my stock, have released from slavery liverate manumitted and set free and by these present Do here by release from slavery liberat manumit and set free my Negro man named Mirida being of the age of thirty years and able to work and gain his sufficient liveahood and maintnance and him the said Negro man Named Mirida I do declare to be hence forth manumitted and discharged

In Testemony whereof I have set my hand and affixed my seal this seventeenth day of March In the year of our Lord 1817

in the presence of us          James Walker
    Gideon Walker
    Katharine                  Mirida

------------------------------

Deed Book I, pp. 157-158 (Film 590,707)

Know all men by these presents that I Christeen Eller the widow of George Eller deceased in the State of Virginia I am now in the County of Monroe and State of Indiana for an in Consideration of two hundred dollars to me in hand paid or used for my benefit through motives of benevolence and humanity I have manumited and do hereby manumit and set free from slavery a certain man of color named Buck aged about fifty years now being in the State of Kentucky Wayne county who is by laws of that State my lawful Slave and I do hereby give grant and release to the said Buck all my right title and claim and all the right title & claim of my heirs executors and administrators in and to the person labour & service of the Said Buck and to any estate or property which he may hereafter acquire or obtain

In witness whereof I have hereunto Set my hand and Seal this tenth day of May in the year of Our Lord Eighteen hundred & forty Two

Attest
    James Pauley          Christeen (X) Eller
    Enentina Ghost

I John Eller a Justice of the Peace of Monroe County and State of Indiana do certify that Christeen Eller of the County of Monroe County and State aforesaid personally appeared before me and Signed Sealed and delivered the within Manumition and acknowledged the same to be her act and deed with her own freee good will without any compulsion or Coersion from any person or persons whatsoever Signed Sealed this day and date above

Given under my hand and Seal this the 10th day of May Eighteen hundred and forty two

        John Eller  Justice of the Peace

State of Indiana  Monroe County

I Wm F. Browning Clerk of the Circuit Court of said County certify that John Eller was at the time of Signing the above certificate an acting Justice of the Peace of Said County duly elected, Commissioned and qualified as Such and that all his acts were entitled to full faith & Credit

Given under my hand and Seal of Said Court August 9th 1845

        Wm F. Browning  Clerk Pro Tem

State of Kentucky  Wayne County Court

I William Simpson clerk of the County Court for the county afsd. do certify that the foregoing deed of Emancipation from Christeen Eller to her Servant Buck together with the certificates thereon was on the 25th day of August 1845 produced to me in my office by the Buck and at his instance and request the same together with this certificate has been duly recorded in my office

Given under my hand the 16th day of January 1846

                    W. Simpson
            By I. N. Sheppard D.C.

## Appendix C: Court Orders

Court Order Book G, p. 125
(Film 591,545)

Wayne County, Kentucky Court
December Term 1859

David Rankin & others

### Petition for division of Slaves

This cause was this day submitted and heard upon the Petition Exhibits on file and the report of the Commissioners filed at the last Term of this Court The Court being sufficiently advised pronounced the following opinions and Judgement. There appearing to be no exception to the Report of the Commissioners afsd. and the Same being inspected by the Court is now approved and Confirmed. And it further appearing that all of the parties interested in the slaves mentioned in the Petition have Joined in the petition for Division It is therefore ordered and adjudged that said Slaves be divided in kind according to the report of the Commissioners aforesaid

It is adjudged that the Petitioners James R. Wilhite hold on Severalty the Slaves allotted to him as follows Lucinda & young child, Garrett, Henry, Bazeal, Charles & Ceasar. And it is further adjudged that said Jas. R. Wilhite pay Samuel W. Gover & wife the sum of Fifty One dollars and fifty six cents with interest at the rate of Six per cent per annum from the date until paid.

Also pay David Rankin and wife the Sum of Fifty One Dollars & 56/100 with like interest from this date. And it is further adjudged that said Wilhite pay David Rankin as Guardian for the infant Petitioners viz Matilda, Wm. R., George T., Samuel B., Thomas C. and Mary Gillespie The Sum of Three Hundred and nine Dollars and thirty eight cents with like interest from this date These Several sums being the Amount of $412.50 which said Wilhite was to pay the other petitioners to equalize them in division made by the Commissioners afsd It is further ordered & adjudged that the Slaves Eliza Bob Morris Sarah and Lewis be held by the petitioners David Rankin & Samuel Gover in their capacity of Executors of Wm. Gillespie decd. and for the use of said Estate under the terms and directions of the Will of Sd. Wm Gillespie

It is further ordered that the petitioner David Rankin hold in Severalty the Slave Louis mentioned in the report afsd., It appearing by the Will of said Gillespie that Samuel W. Gover was to have a negro allotted to him and that the Commissioners afsd. did allot a Slave John to said Gover out of the Estate of Wm Gillespie decd. but not of the Slaves mentioned in the Petition It is now adjudged that said Gover hold said Slave in severalty the share of his wife in the estate of Wm Gillespie however to be charged with the appraised value of said negro towit $1200 Also the Share of David Rankin & wife in the estate of Wm Gillespie is to be charged with the appraised value of the Slave Louis towit $1200

It is further ordered and adjudged that John S. Vanwinkle be allowed the Sum of Fifty Dollars as an Attorney's fee for prosecuting this proceeding which Sum the Clerk is directed to tax as cost in this Suit

It is adjudged that James R. Wilhite pay half of the costs of this proceeding And that David Rankin & Samuel W. Gover pay the other half of the Costs afsd. for which Sum they will be entitled as a Credit in the settlement of this Account as Executors of the Estate of Wm Gillespie

The following books and articles are offered as supplementary reading for the family historian interested in learning more about the institution of slavery as it existed in America. These are but a sampling of the material actually available on this subject, but one can gain a broader and more substantial understanding of the various aspects of slavery through a review of any combination of these publications. No consensus has ever existed regarding the "merits," consequences, realities and characteristics of American slavery, and a wide range of opinions and interpretations can be found even within the works listed below. The reader will want to be aware of these differing points of view and will want to evaluate each of these studies accordingly.

Bancroft, Frederic. Slave-Trading In The Old South. Baltimore: Furst Co., 1931.

Bellamy, Donnie D. "Slavery In Microcosm: Onslow County, North Carolina." Journal of Negro History 62 (October 1977): 339-350.

Berlin, Ira. Slaves without Masters: The Free Negro in the Antebellum South. New York: Pantheon, 1974.

Blassingame, John W. The Slave Community: Plantation Life in the Antebellum South. New York: Oxford University Press, 1972.

_____, ed. Slave Testimony. Baton Rouge: Louisiana State University Press, 1977.

Campbell, Stanley W. The Slave Catchers: Enforcement of the Fugitive Slave Law, 1850-1860. Chapel Hill: University of North Carolina Press, 1970.

Coleman, J. Winston Jr. Slavery Times in Kentucky. Chapel Hill: University of North Carolina Press, 1940.

Currie, James T. "From Slavery To Freedom In Mississippi's Legal System." Journal of Negro History 65 (Spring 1980): 112-125.

Elkins, Stanley M. Slavery: A Problem in American Institutional and Intellectual Life. 3rd ed. Chicago: University of Chicago Press, 1976.

Fogel, Robert W., and Engerman, Stanley L. Time on the Cross: The Economics of Slavery. Boston: Little, Brown & Co., 1974. *The reader will want to be aware of Herbert Gutman's critique of this work.

Genovese, Eugene D. The Political Economy of Slavery: Studies in the Economy and Society of the Slave South. New York: Pantheon, 1965.

_____. Roll Jordan Roll: The World The Slaves Made. New York: Vintage Books, 1976.

Guild, June Purcell. Black Laws of Virginia. 1936, reprint ed. New York: Negro Universities Press, 1969.

Gutman, Herbert G. The Black Family In Slavery and Freedom, 1750-1925. New York: Pantheon Books, 1976.

_____. Slavery and the Numbers Game: A Critique of Time on the Cross. Chicago: University of Illinois Press, 1975.

Harrison, Lowell H. "Memories of Slavery Days In Kentucky." Filson Club History Quarterly 47 (July 1973): 242-258.

McDougle, Ivan E. Slavery In Kentucky. Ph.D. dissertation, Clark University, 1918. reprint Westport, Conn.: Negro Universities Press, 1970.

Miller, Elinor, and Genovese, Eugene D., ed. Plantation, Town and County. Chicago: University of Illinois Press, 1974.

Mohr, Clarence L. "Slavery in Oglethorpe County, Georgia." Phylon 33 (Spring 1972): 4-21.

Mooney, Chase C. Slavery in Tennessee. Bloomington, IN.: Indiana University Press, 1957.

Owens, Leslie Howard. This Species of Property: Slave Life and Culture in the Old South. New York: Oxford University Press, 1976.

Phifer, E. W. "Slavery in Microcosm: Burke County, North Carolina." Journal of Southern History XXVIII (May 1962): 137-160.

Phillips, Ulrich B. American Negro Slavery: A Survey of the Supply, Employment and Control of Negro Labor as Determined by the Plantation Regime. New York: D. Appleton, 1918. *Although this early work has fallen into disfavor in more recent times, it continues to be a work of importance because it has served as a catalyst for many succeeding studies.

Pollard, Leslie J. "Aging and Slavery: A Gerontological Perspective." Journal of Negro History 66 (Fall 1981): 228-234.

Ramsdell, Charles W. "The Natural Limits of Slavery Expansion." Mississippi Valley Historical Review XVI (1929): 151-171.

Rawick, George P. From Sundown to Sunup: The Making of the Black Community. Westport, Conn.: Greenwood Publishing Co., 1972.

Rivers, Larry E. "Slavery In Microcosm: Leon County, Florida." Journal of Negro History 66 (Fall 1981): 235-245.

Scarpino, Philip V. "Slavery in Callaway County, Missouri: 1845-1855." Missouri Historical Review 71 (October 1976, April 1977): 22-43, 266-283.

Schweninger, Loren. "A Slave Family In the Ante-Bellum South." Journal of Negro History 60 (January 1975): 29-44.

Smith, John David. "The Recruitment of Negro Soldiers In Kentucky, 1863-1865." The Register of the Kentucky Historical Society 72 (October 1974): 364-390.

Stampp, Kenneth M. The Peculiar Institution: Slavery In the Ante-Bellum South. New York: Alfred A. Knopf, 1956.

Steely, Will Fank. "The Established Churches and Slavery, 1850-1860." The Register of the Kentucky Historical Society 55 (April 1957): 97-104.

Sydnor, Charles S. Slavery In Mississippi. 1933. reprint ed. New York: American Historical Association, 1965.

Trexler, Harrison A. "Slavery in Missouri Territory." Missouri Historical Review 3 (April 1909): 179-198.

Waughan, Alden T. "Blacks in Virginia: A Note on the First Decade." William and Mary Quarterly, Third Series, 29 (July 1972): 469-478.

Wamble, Gaston Hugh. "Negroes and Missouri Protestant Churches Before and After the Civil War." Missouri Historical Review 61 (April 1967): 321-347.

Many of these books contain their own more exhaustive bibliographies and offer the reader a thorough historiography on slavery.

BIBLIOGRAPHY

## Primary Data

1810-1900 U.S. Population Census, Wayne
County, Kentucky.
1850-1860 U.S. Slave Schedule Censuses,
Wayne County, Kentucky.
1850 U.S. Mortality Schedule Census,
Wayne County, Kentucky.
U. S. Bureau of the Census Statistics of
United States, 1860. Washington,
D.C.: Government Printing Office,
1866.
Ninth Census of the United States, 1870:
Population and Social Statistics.
Washington, D.C.: Government Printing
Office, 1872.
Compendium of the Tenth Census of the
United States, 1880. Washington,
D.C.: Government Printing Office,
1883.
Compendium of the Eleventh Census, 1890,
Part II. Washington, D.C.: Govern-
ment Printing Office, 1894.
Census Report: Twelfth Census of the
United States, 1900. Washington,
D.C.: U.S. Census Office, 1902.
Wayne County Appraisements & Inven-
tories: Films 591,562 - 591,548
(1816-1907).
Wayne County Probate Records: Film
591,542 (1802-1909).
Wayne County Guardian Bonds: Films
591,599 - 591,560 (1853-1904).
Wayne County Land & Property Deed Books:
Film 590,700 General Index
Films 590,703-590,711 Books A-R (1800
-1875)
Films 591,531-591,540 (1874-1909)
Wayne County Marriage Bonds:
Film 591,549 General Index to Mar-
riages, (1801-1869)
Films 591,550-591,558 Marriages,
(1801-1900).

Wayne County Vital Statistics:
Film 216,842 item 4, Births, Deaths,
Marriages: (1852-1859)
Film 174,932 Births, (1874)
Film 174,935 Births, (1878)
Film 174,938 Deaths, (1874)
Film 174,939 Deaths, (1878).
Wayne County Tax Books:
Films 008,269 - 008,273 (1808-1875).

*The films listed in the bibliography
refer to microfilm copies of original
documents. Films can be found at the
LDS Genealogical Society Library in Salt
Lake City, Utah.

## Wayne County, Kentucky

Boertman, C. Stewart. The Sequence of
the Occupance In Wayne County, Ken
tucky: An Historical Study. Ph.D.
dissertation, University of Michigan,
1934.
Bork, June Baldwin. Wayne County,
Kentucky: Vital Records. 3 vols.
Huntigton Beach, Calif.: By the Aut-
hor, 1973.
Coffey, Bennie, and Coffey, Juanita.
Cemeteries of Wayne County, Kentucky.
Monticello, Ky.: Lakeview Printing,
Inc., 1982.
Johnson, Augusta Phillips. A Century of
Wayne County, Kentucky, 1800-1900.
Louisville: Standard Printing Co.,
1939.
Sexton, Jacqueline Coffey. The Coffeys
of Wayne County. Monticello, Ky: By
the Author, 1974.
Vickery, Ala Shearer, and Simpson,
Elizabeth. Deeds and Records Per-
taining to Shearer Valley Church of

Christ. Monticello, Ky.: By the Authors, 1975.

Walker, Garnet. Pleasant Vineyards: The Baptist Churches of Wayne County. Monticello, Ky.: By the Author, 1960. (Film 728,097 item 9, LDS Library).


## Historical References

Bancroft, Frederic. Slave-Trading In The Old South. Baltimore: Furst Co., 1931.

Billington, Ray Allen, and Ridge, Martin. Westward Expansion. 5th ed. New York: MacMillan Publishing Co., 1982.

Blassingame, John W. The Slave Community: Plantation Life in the Antebellum South. New York: Oxford University Press, 1972.

_____, ed. Slave Testimony. Baton Rouge: Louisiana State University Press, 1977.

Douglass, Frederick. Life and Times of Frederick Douglass. Hartford, Conn.: Park Publishing Co., 1881.

Elkins, Stanley M. Slavery: A Problem in American Institutional and Intellectual Life. 3rd ed. Chicago: University of Chicago Press, 1976.

Genovese, Eugene D. The Political Economy of Slavery: Studies in the Economy and Society of the Slave South. New York: Pantheon, 1965.

_____. Roll Jordan Roll: The World The Slaves Made. New York: Vintage Books, 1976.

Gutman, Herbert G. The Black Family In Slavery and Freedom, 1750-1925. New York: Pantheon Books, 1976.

_____. Slavery and the Numbers Game: A Critique of Time on the Cross. Chicago: University of Illinois Press, 1975.

McDougle, Ivan E. Slavery In Kentucky. Ph. D. dissertation, Clark University. 1918. Reprint ed. Westport, Conn.: Negro Universities Press, 1970.

Mohr, Clarence L. "Slavery in Oglethorpe County, Georgia." Phylon 33 (Spring 1972): 4-21.

Smith, John David. "The Recruitment of Negro Soldiers In Kentucky, 1863-

1865." The Register of the Kentucky Historical Society 72 (October 1974): 364-390.

Stampp, Kenneth M. The Peculiar Institution: Slavery In the Ante-Bellum South. New York: Alfred A. Knopf, 1956.

Steely, Will Frank. "The Established Churches and Slavery, 1850-1860." The Register of the Kentucky Historical Society 55 (April 1957): 97-104.

Sydnor, Charles S. Slavery In Mississippi. 1933. Reprint ed. New York: American Historical Association, 1965.

Wamble, Gaston Hugh. "Negroes and Missouri Protestant Churches Before and After the Civil War." Missouri Historical Review 61 (April 1967): 321-347.


## Genealogy

Beard, Timothy F. How to Find Your Family Roots. New York: McGraw-Hill Book Co., 1977.

Black Studies Microfilm Catalogue. Washington, D.C.: National Archives and Records Service, 1971.

Blockson, Charles L., and Fry, Ron. Black Genealogy. Englewood Cliffs, N.J.: Prentice-Hall, Inc., 1977.

Bluegrass Roots, vol. X, no. 2 (Summer 1983): 64.

Doane, Gilbert H., and Bell, James B. Searching for Your Ancestors. Minneapolis: University of Minn. Press, 1980.

Everly, Elaine C. "Marriage Registers of Freedmen." Prologue: Journal of the National Archives 5 (Fall 1973): 150-154.

Everton, George B. Sr., ed. The Handy Book For Genealogists. 7th ed. Logan, Utah: Everton Publishers, Inc., 1981.

Haley, Alex. Roots. Garden City, N.Y.: Doubleday, 1976.

Hilton, Suzanne. Who Do You Think You Are? Digging For Your Family Roots. Philadelphia: Westminster Press, 1976.

Journal of Afro-American Historical and Genealogical Society. Washington,

D.C.: Afro-American Historical and Genealogical Society (PO Box 13086, T Street Station, Washington, D.C. 20009).

Kirkham, E. Kay. A Survey of American Census Schedules. 2nd ed. Provo, Utah: Stevenson's Genealaogical Center, 1972.

List of Black Servicemen Compiled from the War Department Collection of Revolutionary War Records. Washington, D.C.: National Archives and Records Service, 1978.

McBride, Ransom. "Searching for the Past of the North Carolina Black Family." North Carolina Genealogical Society Journal, vol. ix, no. 2 (May 1983): 66-77.

Okihiro, Gary Y. "Oral History and the Writing of Ethnic History: A Reconnaissance into Method and Theory." Oral History Review 9 (1981): 27-46.

Puckett, Newbell Niles, and Heller, Murray, ed. Black Names in America: Origins and Usage. Boston: G.K. Hall and Co., 1975.

"Records of Black Americans." Guide to Genealogical Research in the National Archives. Washington, D.C.: National Archives and Records Service, 1982.

Roderick, Thomas H. "Negro Genealogy." American Genealogist 47 (1971): 88-91.

Rose, James, and Eichnolz, Alice. Black Genesis. Detroit: Gale Research Co., 1978.

Rubincam, Milton, ed. Genealogical Research: Methods and Sources. 2 vols. Revised ed., Washington, D.C.: American Society of Genealogists, 1980.

_____. "Genealogy For All People." National Genealogical Society Quarterly 66 (December 1978): 243-251.

Schatz, Walter, ed. Directory of Afro-American Resources. New York: R.R. Bowker, 1980.

Schriner-Yantis, Netti, ed. Genealogical & Local History Books in Print. 3rd ed. Springfield, Virginia: Genealogical Books in Print, 1981.

Shockley, Ann. "Oral History: Research Tool for Black History." Negro History Bulletin, vol. 41, no. 11 (Jan.-Feb. 1978).

Walker, James D. Black Genealogy: How to Begin. Athens, Georgia: University of Georgia Center for Continuing Education, 1977.

Westin, Jeane Eddy. Finding Your Roots: How Every American Can Trace His Ancestors. Los Angeles: J.P. Tarcher, Inc., 1977.

Wright, George C. "Oral History and the Search for the Black Past in Kentucky." Oral History Review 10 (1982): 73-91.

Wright, Norman E. Preserving Your American Heritage. Provo, Utah: Brigham Young University Press, 1981.

Young, Tommie M. "Ten Steps in Rooting Out the Past of the Black Family." North Carolina Genealogical Society Journal, vol. vi, no. 3 (August 1981): 150-161.